BARTLETT DESIGNS

BARTLETT DESIGNS

SPECULATING WITH ARCHITECTURE

Edited by
Laura Allen, Iain Borden, Nadia O'Hare and Neil Spiller

A John Wiley and Sons, Ltd, Publication

Executive Commissioning Editor: Helen Castle
Project Editor: Miriam Swift
Publishing Assistant: Calver Lezama

ISBN 978-0-470-68283-8 (hb)
ISBN 978-0-470-68282-1 (pb)

Cover design, page design and layouts by Mikkel Lundsager Hansen
Art Direction by Andersen M Studio
Cover, Summer Show and models by Kyle Buchanan and Sara Shafiei:
photographs by Richard Stonehouse
All other images: individual authors

Printed in Italy by Conti Tipocolor

Acknowledgements

The editors would like to thank everyone at Wiley for their advice and support in producing this book, along with graphic designer Martin Andersen. Particular gratitude is also due to UCL Futures, who very generously supported the publication financially. Above all, we offer our immense and unreserved thanks to all of the staff and students who contributed to *Bartlett Designs*, without whose tremendous efforts and creativity none of this would have been possible.

Contents

Bartlett Designs

Iain Borden

British architectural education began at University College London (UCL) in 1841. Named later in the 19th century after its benefactor, the engineer and construction contractor Sir Herbert Bartlett, the UCL Bartlett has gone on to become one of the most prestigious and famous schools of architecture, construction and planning in the world. Today, over 250 staff and more than 1,400 students research, teach and study a myriad of subjects and specialisms right across the built environment field. Largest of all of these is the UCL Bartlett School of Architecture – with over 130 staff and 850 students exploring the design, history, theory, technology and profession of architecture. Courses range from those for students dedicated to becoming architects to others with more specialist areas of focus.

Across all of these programmes runs one central concern: a simple yet profound and constant questioning as to what architecture might be. This is what drives both staff and students alike – not what architecture is already understood to be, or how it is already created and practised, but what it could be, along with the attendant pursuit of what we might do in order to understand, engage with and ultimately create that potential architecture.

As apparently simple as this line of questioning might be, the answers are, of course, considerably more complex in nature. In previous eras of its history, the Bartlett's approach to architecture might even have considered that a certain and finite answer might be found, as in the 1960s and in Richard Llewellyn-Davies' positioning of architecture within the teamwork and decision-making nexus of the construction industry and environmental design. Yet, in the 1990s, these answers became at once more complex, and in two important ways. First, with the arrival of Peter Cook (who stayed with the School for over a decade) and a whole swathe of young architect-designers, the focus on architecture at the Bartlett was fundamentally shifted to that of design. Second, with the rapidly developing interests of Bartlett staff in such things as: architectural technology, art practice, climate change, digital media, fabrication, history, landscape, theory and urbanism, came all manner of concerns to do with the digital, environmental, experiential, representational, socio-political and technological nature of architecture, either in terms of architect-designed projects or in more everyday spaces and structures.

In the Cook-oriented 1990s, as showcased in our previous book of student work, *Bartlett Book of Ideas* (1999), these two areas of development are much in evidence but, perhaps sometimes, run alongside each other rather than clearly engaging in some kind of interactive dialogue. In this book, *Bartlett Designs*, a more common project has now clearly emerged. Over the last 10 years, when the new breed of teachers and students have been given free rein to develop deeper agendas, the Bartlett has moved to a much more interdisciplinary and integrative approach to architecture, where many of the concerns with technology, digital media, history and theory are equally commonplace in the design studio, and, vice versa, where many of the concerns of the design studio are equally commonplace in the seminar room and workshop. Indeed, for the Bartlett's staff and students, one could say that such distinctions are no longer of central concern, nor, in many cases, do they operate at all. What matters now is not so much the medium, but the overall aim that architecture and how we go about architecture, as substance and as practice, are both continually questioned for its possibilities.

The student projects in this book are hugely wide-ranging in their ideas – encompassing all manner of concepts, technologies, systems, networks, philosophies and politics – as well as being determinedly focused on the realisation of these ideas in and through design. What emerges, therefore, is a set of intensive research agendas that utilise design as both the subject and the method by which this research is conducted. This is a broad and intensively investigated enquiry into the possibilities for architecture.

So what are these possibilities for architecture? What might be seen from the extraordinary range of student projects contained within *Bartlett Designs*? Here are 10 conjectures.

1 Architecture As Design

Too often, the real achievement of architecture is held to be evident only through quantities, figures, contexts and calculations, where design is thought to act as an adjunct, being the 'result' of, or 'following on from', other, more quantifiable considerations. The Bartlett wholly rejects such assertions, believing instead that not only is design central to the operation of architectural education but that much of what some believe can be taught only in the lecture room (structures, technology,

Clockwise from right:
Sara Shafiei, **'Magicians' Theatre, Rome'**
Johan Berglund, **'A Colourworks,
Royal Victoria Docks, London'**
John Ashton, **'Inhabiting Infrastructures, Levittown'**
Anthony Lau, **'Floating City 2030'**

Offshore Living

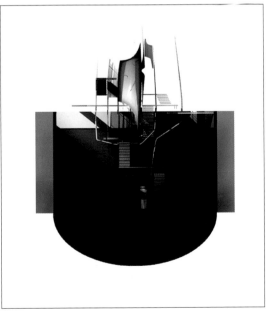

9

Horse Race Festival

Above: Dimitrios Argyros, **'Luxor by Horse'**
Bottom left: Kyle Buchanan, **'Instrumental Architectures'**
Bottom right: Yumi Saito, **'Capacitor, Lea Valley, London'**

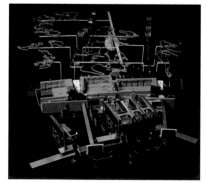

culture, professionalism) can in fact be embedded directly in the design process itself.

This position speaks to the very heart of architecture, for it sees that one of the truly creative contributions of architecture is in the design process itself, a place where all manner of other hugely complex concerns are not only brought together, not only resolved, but are creatively combined to produce a wholly unique addition to the process of building, postulating, inventing and producing architecture. In Sara Shafiei's 'Magicians' Theatre, Rome project, for example, concerns with anamorphosis, perspective, illusion and performance are all brought together in a single 3-D proposition and constructed through a series of intricately wrought laser-cut models. The projects in this book, therefore, propose something architectural – they do not speculate purely at a theoretical, philosophical or conjectural level about architecture, but undertake to suggest a project which in some shape or form actually envisages how architecture might be.

2 Architecture Through Design

As this suggests, at the Bartlett many aspects of architecture – such as structures, technology, environmental factors, history and theory – have been investigated directly through the students' own design projects. In many cases, this increasingly takes the form of explorations of a particular part of architecture through the design of those projects. This kind of approach, of course, pursues a myriad of paths and directions and adopts a similarly bewildering range of forms and appearances. It ranges from the sociological and anthropological concerns of Caspar Rodgers' 'Mobile Appliances for the Hells Angels', to the literary focus of Fiona Sheppard's 'Stolen Kiss', to the bio-scientific investigations of Sacha Leong's 'Biotechnology of Breakfast' and Ryan Martin's 'Efflorescent Drawing Device', to the interdisciplinary interests (dealing, inter alia, with optics, relativity, mythology, symbolism and history) of Tim Norman's magnificent study, 'Cosmic House'.

3 Architecture For Design

Embedded in such processes and projects are a whole series of other concerns related to becoming a creative professional, not least those to do with what are sometimes referred to as competences, skills and training. These range from the obvious generic skills of reading, writing, calculating, drawing and communicating, to the more specific areas of architectural knowledge concerning professional requirements and contexts, legislation, structures and basic historical facts, and skills such as model-making, drawing protocols, image manipulation and visualisation of all kinds.

As already argued above, such processes – as seemingly prosaic as they might appear – do not need to be treated normatively or uncreatively. This is part of almost every good student project – a critical self-reflection not just on what has been proposed, but how and why that proposition has been constructed – and it perhaps reaches its apogee in the work of PhD students, where such considerations are highly explicit. In the architectural design thesis 'Digital Poetics' by Marjan Colletti, pure parametric and algorithmic computerised architecture is rejected in favour of a poetic digital avant-garde that is equally developed through 3-D software and Computer Numerically Controlled (CNC), Rapid Prototyping (CRP) and Computer-Aided Design and Computer-Aided Manufacture (CAD-CAM) technologies. Similarly, in the history and theory thesis by Lilian Chee, 'Intimate Encounter', there is an equal focus on methodology, and this time on the role of evidence – such as anecdotes, fictions, rumour, gossip and trivia – in the construction of alternative architectural histories.

4 Architecture is Multi-Disciplinary and Specialist

Architecture is made by many people, and therefore the architect has almost never worked completely alone. It is, of course, very difficult to replicate the conditions of a large (or even a small) architectural practice within an architecture school, even if one wished to do so. The Bartlett however, by virtue of being based in London – one of the great design centres of the world – is able to draw on the expertise of an enormous range of specialist tutors, offering all manner of advice ranging from: environmental concerns with heat, air pollution, sound and sustainability through planning, urban design, history, theory, fabrication, manufacture, structures and materials, right through to digital concerns with cybernetics, interaction design, audio, video, virtuality and computational design.

Without such specialist input, work such as the 'Pie Shop, Bloomsbury, London' by Ian Laurence, Karl Normanton and Frances Taylor (and informed by a large team of tutors and other specialist experts), would be impossible. Delving into this project reveals an extraordinarily intense enquiry into almost every aspect of the production and selling of food, from architectural structures and technology to environmental systems and food handling – all wrapped up in (and explored through) an exquisitely presented integrative set of designs, studies and reports.

5 Architecture is Solution

So what do such explorations achieve? What contribution do these design projects make to the world?

Recently UCL has set the whole university four 'grand challenges' regarding research: global health (beyond malaria and HIV to all aspects of medical need across the world); sustainable cities (not only climate change and environmental responsibility but the much more complex social, cultural and economic sustainability and reproducibility of our built environment); intercultural interaction (how societies, groups and individuals understand, respect and live with each other); and well-being (all of the qualities of everyday life that make us truly alive, from political rights to personal love, from enjoyment of the arts to expressions of ideas).

It would be naïve in the extreme to expect any one university – still less any one architecture school, programme or student – to somehow solve such fundamental problems. Yet very definite and worthwhile solutions can indeed be proposed, if not immediately enacted, by design projects. To give but one example in relation to global health, the project by Owen Jones makes a very real suggestion. Faced with an ever-increasing demand for morphine-based pain-killing drugs both in the UK's National Health Service (NHS) and elsewhere in the world, the 'Opium Refinery, London' scheme proposes a complete system for the cultivation (on barges floating out on the River Thames), refinement (in the refinery itself), security (through a complex series of vault-like constrictions) and also display (through a series of visitor routes) of opium production. Leaving aside the considerable architectural quality of the project, the scheme would potentially save the UK's NHS millions of pounds a year, as well as help to relieve the suffering of thousands of patients.

6 Architecture is Critical

As the 'Opium Refinery' project suggests, architecture is a form of critical thinking in visual and spatial terms. When explored with ambition, creativity and intellect, then embedded in it – thought through it – is a whole series of critical reflections on what our world might be.

With reference to another of UCL's grand challenges – sustainable cities – many Bartlett design projects meet such

concerns head on. One of our graduate teaching groups explored the architectural and urban design of the town of 'Hubbert Curve' (named after geoscientist M King Hubbert who predicted that available fossil fuel reserves would be dramatically reduced by 2050 and fully depleted by 2200). In this stimulating proposition, each student's project – see John Ashton's 'Inhabiting Infrastructures, Levittown' is included in this book – has a reciprocal relationship with at least three other projects in the town. As they explain: 'Sustainable, the town trades and exchanges with its environment; one expands and contracts, receives and donates, adapts and adjusts, in response to the other. Self-sufficient, the town generates its own energy; each building produces its own energy and creates an excess that serves the general needs of the town. Discursive, the town encourages social and political engagement, and the interaction of public and private lives. Independent, the town learns from earlier centuries as well as those more recent, inventing and adapting narratives, histories and myths that define its character. Seasonal, the town is responsive to its climate and site, creating conditions that are conducive to its survival and growth.' In a similar environmentally-oriented project, this time pursued as a full-scale installation, Tim Barwell's 'Resonant Observatory, UCL' responds to climatic changes and renders them visible to the public in a peculiarly delightful performance.

7 Architecture is Propositional

These are serious propositions, and they contain more than a little sense of the world outside the university- and studio-based project. They are, in many ways, 'as if' projects, designs which imagine a world where these projects really are built and realised. They carry with them the force and ambition of being actual, achievable proposals. And yet, simultaneously, they also do the opposite – which is to fully understand that the true context of the university and the studio is not to mimic the world of real developers, real money, real sites, real people, for to do so could (and perhaps necessarily would) constrain the possibility of imagining and proposing something more innovative. Hence the kind of project which makes a virtue out of this unreality, works in relation to the real and enacts a critical and propositional tension between the two.

Here, the 'as if' becomes 'what if?' What if we were to create Ben Ridley's 'Icelandic Parliament, Thingvellir' and help to confront issues of migration, national identity and personal health, or Christian Kerrigan's 'Ship Cultivation, Epping

Forest, London' project and try to grow architecture, or Dean Pike's 'Camden Market Council' and deal with matters of local government, or Yumi Saito's 'Capacitor, Lea Valley, London' and create architecture of pure pleasure, or Anthony Lau's 'Floating City 2030' and start to address issues of rising sea levels, housing, energy supply and industrial waste?

What if we were to build something like this, what if it were to be enacted? Perhaps not as a truly realisable proposition, but as a possibility of architecture. This, then, is the propositional nature of architecture, a place for asking questions as much as finding solutions, but doing so in a way that always conveys some kind of explorative and potential connection between what can be done, what might be done, what should be done and what imaginably could be done.

8 Architecture is Non-Discursive

In all of this, it is worth bearing in mind that architecture frequently approaches such investigations in a way that does not rely on words: its discourse is often not verbal, does not rely on and cannot always be reduced to words. Architecture is visual and spatial, and, furthermore, its discourse is often non-discursive, in that it is often not codified within broadly held sets of theories or conventions as to how that visuality and spatiality might be conceived or communicated.

Unfortunately, as a result of this unique undertaking, too often the hugely ambitious and fantastic investigations undertaken in visual and spatial form within architecture are dismissed as purely that – 'merely' shapes, surfaces and spaces. To denigrate architecture in this way is to miss the point, to fail to see one of the essential characteristics of architecture, that of its capacity to think, critique, propose and enact through lines, models, spaces, forms. And to dismiss architectural invention as being no more than visual and spatial play would be akin to brushing aside literature for being no more than the articulation of verbs and adjectives, letters and words, keyboards and pens.

So in looking at some of the complex designs in this book, one must realise that they are indeed visual and spatial thinking, not just formal invention. In projects such as Johan Berglund's 'A Colourworks, Royal Victoria Docks, London', we find an investigation into light, vision, materiality and landscape that is not reducible to words, that is not 'represented' just in visual terms but is thought through in a highly considered sequence of precisely directed visual and spatial studies. Similar attitudes to the power of non-verbal thinking can be found in the many

'Installation Projects' produced every year by first year students in BSc Architecture, as in Ben Olszyna-Marzys' treatment of post-industrial life in 'London After the Rain', and in Joerg Majer's curious constructed archive of architecture in 'Gulliver'. And if, in some way, the exact meaning of such projects is not always immediately evident, well that is in the nature of their architectural thought, deliberately giving space to the viewer's own reaction and contemplation as much as to the author's own intentions.

9 Architecture is Discursive

And yet, of course, at other times architecture can also be textual, can also be related to discourses of all kinds. Very often this occurs in words, in the texts written, from the simple project descriptions used in this book, to massively complex and detailed arguments contained in PhD theses. Hence, for example, the kind of erudite scholarship of Jacob Paskins' 'Aural Experience' MA Architectural History dissertation, or Josie Kane's history PhD, 'Whirl of Wonders!', which explicates architecture, technology and social characteristics of these fantastic structures. Hence also more design-related explorations such as John Puttick's truly extraordinary 'Land of Scattered Seeds' which, through both design and text, explores questions of narrative, personal character, economics and environmental growth.

10 Architecture Brings Alive

Whatever the solutions and critical questions proffered in architectural design and textual projects alike, one must also bear in mind that the great problems facing us today are not there just to be solved immediately, questioned or even identified through direct confrontation. Much of the power and significance of architecture comes from the many subtle and pervasive ways by which it can enter into our everyday lives and cultural meanings.

To respond to the last three of UCL's grand challenges – sustainable cities, intercultural interaction and well-being – one can see how many of the projects in *Bartlett Designs* create new agendas for architectural aesthetics and representation, seeking somehow not to remove or eradicate these grand challenges, but to raise our consciousness of them, and indeed to bring our concerns with them in to our visual and spatial world. Nowhere perhaps, is this of greater importance than in the ways in which concerns with global warming and environmental change are brought alive – given real cultural depth and longevity – through

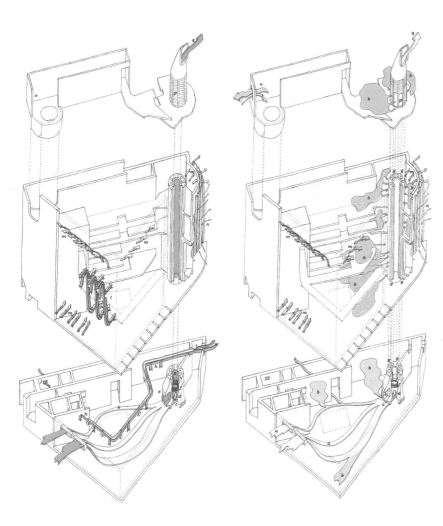

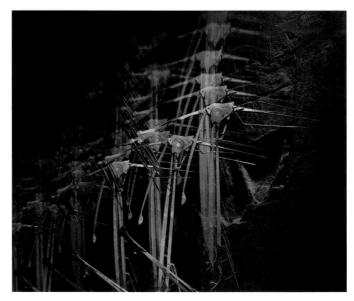

 Bloomsbury Pie Shop:
Heating, Cooling and Ventilation:
Summer: Day

a Fresh air ...
b ... drawn through interior for ventilation ...
c ... is used for combustion.
d Gas: on
e Oven: hot
f Stainless steel heat exchange coil (distilled water):
    flow rate: high
g Insulated non-condensing flue
h Mechanical ventilation: on
i Heat exchanger
j WC mechanical ventilation
k Underfloor heating
l Heat exchanger ventilation alembics: on
m Pie dish window vents: open
n Ipe cladding: air gap
o Wet area mechanical extraction
p Insulated panel: closed
q Flue gas exit

 Bloomsbury Pie Shop:
Heating, Cooling and Ventilation:
Summer: Night

a Fresh air is drawn through interior
b Built up heat is gradually absorbed
c Air is mechanically drawn through flues to cool chimney mass.
d Gas: off
e Oven: cooling
f Stainless steel heat exchange coil (distilled water): flow rate: still
g Uninsulated condensing flue
h Mechanical ventilation: off
i Heat exchanger
j WC mechanical ventilation
k Underfloor heating
l Heat exchanger ventilation alembics: off
m Pie dish window vents: open
n Ipe cladding: air gap
o Wet area mechanical extraction
p Insulated panel: lifted
q Flue gas exit

Left: Ian Laurence, Karl Normanton and Frances Taylor,
'Pie Shop, Bloomsbury, London'
Top: Tim Barwell, **'Resonant Observatory, UCL'**
Bottom: Ryan Martin, **'Efflorescent Drawing Device'**

14

architecture's capacity to embed such concerns in different social and urban situations. Thus in Kyle Buchanan's 'Instrumental Architectures' propositions, one sees a new architecture of vision, a project that responds to the landscape, the horizon and the tides of the River Thames – that is, an architecture which both reflects and helps to engender a deeper and more varied appreciation of our natural and artificial landscape. Similarly, in Dimitrios Argyros' 'Luxor by Horse' we have a project which proposes an eco-friendly and sustainable transport system of horse-and-carriage for Luxor's city centre; not just to alleviate problems with congestion, pollution and employment, but also to create a whole attitude to urban living which incorporates within it concerns with sustainability and the environment.

In such projects, architecture brings things alive, entering into everyday worlds of design, experience, meaning, actuality and possibility. It is here, I feel, that architecture finds its most pertinent value and resonance.

This has not been an easy book to construct. Well over 100 student projects have been selected by the editors from nominations proposed by all of our current staff. This final selection seeks to represent the very best-of-the-best from over 10,000 pieces of student work produced in the Bartlett over the last decade. We would, of course, have liked to include work by many, many more students – and the curious reader might like to see our series of annual *Catalogue* publications, or website, for a window on to numerous other projects.

The work contained in *Bartlett Designs* is drawn from across the School, from undergraduate and graduate programmes alike. Each project is given a page or more, but it is worth pointing out that in each case the author has very often produced scores if not hundreds of other drawings and explorations, which we simply do not have the space to reproduce in full.

Nonetheless, we hope that these highly selective images and projects show something of the incredible diversity, ambition and depth of work that is undertaken every year at the UCL Bartlett School of Architecture. To help explicate each project, we include a brief description. We have also included eight short essays, each written by two or more members of staff, and each of which sets out one of the many tendencies and preoccupations of the School. We have not tried to map these essays against a particular set of projects, for in many cases their positions resonate across a great range of student work, and vice versa.

Above all, this is a celebration of the students' very considerable achievements. We hope that *Bartlett Designs* presents something of this work's hugely ambitious architecture – solving, questioning, proposing and bringing alive, as well as creating what is very often truly fabulous, wondrous and beautiful speculation.

Christian Kerrigan, **'Ship Cultivation, Epping Forest, London'**

A Colourworks, Royal Victoria Docks, London

Johan Berglund
Diploma Architecture (2005)
Tutors: *Niall McLaughlin* and *Yeoryia Manolopoulou*

A neglected piece of land next to the Royal Victoria Graving Dock in east London is imagined as a new paint laboratory with studios and accommodation for resident artists. The proposal responds to the site's history of material refinement, and experiments with how natural light can inventively penetrate otherwise extremely dark spaces. Techniques used in the history of painting, such as the chiaroscuro paintings of Caravaggio, the slashed canvases of Francis Bacon and the convex lenses used by the Renaissance painters to capture light and to magnify and distort views, inspire the design of four distinct rooms for painting. One space folds into another creating a cinematic sequence. Below ground level, an empty dry dock acts as a large sunken courtyard, the centre of gravity for all the meticulously designed passages and chambers above.

The project is concerned with the line where ground meets water (metaphorically as well as physically), with the experience of light and with the powerful presence of the void as manifested within the dry dock. Pigment, colour, oil, water and weather are filtered and celebrated through the architecture. Leaks of pigments from the making of colour and from the gradual weathering of the facades modify the building and its surroundings – an ever-changing landscape painting on the ground.

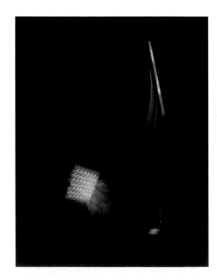

All the Fun of the Circus

David Roy
Diploma Architecture (2005)
Tutors: *John Puttick* and *Peter Szczepaniak*

A highly narrative project, 'All the Fun of the Circus' investigates the extremely peculiar mobile world of a travelling Russian circus. The idiosyncratic proposal envisages a peripatetic train, where each carriage is designed according to the specific personality and profession of its occupant – clown, trapeze artist, and so on. As the narrative unfolds, different personal relationships are formed, leading to hybrid architectural conditions and spaces being constructed. The whole project is beautifully realised through a series of delicately and finely crafted models.

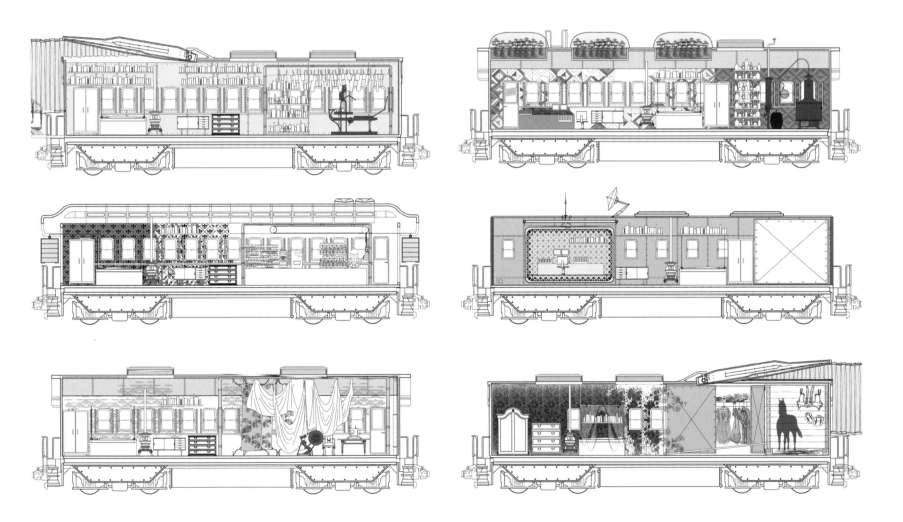

Allegorical House and Registry Office, Mexico City

Considered both a traitor and the mother of contemporary Mexico, due to her role as interpreter and mistress of conquistador Hernán Cortés, La Malinche is the inspiration behind this project. La Malinche's allegorical house merges a physical model with film in order to describe water as an architectural material. Water, or its absence, is of special significance to Mexico City, because the Spanish established the contemporary capital after draining the original lake city.

Costa Elia
BSc Architecture (2007)
Tutors: *Penelope Haralambidou* and *Eduardo Rosa*

Auction House, London

Tom Holberton
BSc Architecture (2002)
Tutors: *Penelope Haralambidou* and *Eduardo Rosa*

The 'Auction House' is a building in two halves, separated by the River Thames. Sited alongside the old Blackfriars Bridge, the structure establishes an immaterial connection between north and south London. The first half, on the south bank, contains the exhibition hall, which is exposed to the city and designed as a new public space. The second half, on the north bank, contains a restaurant, which is designed as an exclusive and secluded space where potential buyers make their offers. Through the innovative application of polarised light, the building introduces notions of noise, participation and accident. Implicit in the project are key questions such as those addressing the relationship between public and private spaces, and the role that architecture can play as mediated experience, thus bridging the gap between, on the one hand, the tangible and the material and, on the other hand, the invisible and the extraordinary.

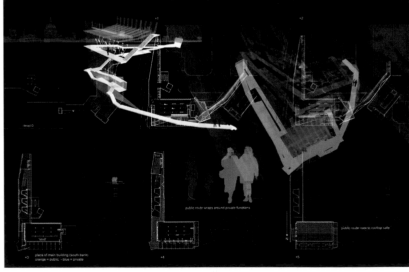

Jacob Paskins
MA Architectural History (2008)
Supervisor: *Iain Borden*

This masters dissertation – 'The Aural Experience of Travelling on the London Underground' – is an investigation into sound on the London Underground today. The Tube is a noisy place: a survey by the UCL Audiology unit recorded noise levels on the Victoria line higher than those of a pneumatic drill – enough to damage hearing. But what are the social, physical and spatial implications of our daily sound-filled journey underneath the city?

A twist on the travel genre, the dissertation is structured along the route of a daily Tube journey. Rather than attempting a general account of sound on the entire network, it focuses on aural circumstances particular to the stations and trains along a specific route. While the route takes in the two most recent additions to the Tube network – the Victoria and Jubilee lines – the design of each, both exploiting the most modern techniques of its day, but separated by three decades, has fundamentally different approaches to sound.

Users of noise-reducing headphones on the Victoria line attempt to maintain a private existence free from the sound of the public transport, despite maintaining a visual awareness of the carriage. This paradoxical territorialisation blurs the clear distinction between home and travel space: the inside and outside created by the 'sonic bridge' of the artificial silence or music on the headphones. Choosing to listen to the sound of the train's engine and rumble through the tunnel is a type of relationship with the city that unsettles fixed notions of where public and private space is located. The body's passage through the city, enhanced by listening, unsettles other navigational practices that are based on the 'spatial and visual order of the city' (Jean-Paul Thibaud). Unlike following maps, plans and signs – trains this way – guiding oneself through the station by listening to its sound becomes both a mental and a physical exercise that 'structures and articulates the experience and understanding of space' (Juhani Pallasmaa). In doing so, listening to architecture, detecting the temporal and spatial progress of a journey by responding to an inbuilt memory of sound – even the asynchronous sound of a passing escape shaft – further unsettles fixed typologies of built form such as interior and exterior.

Bankrupts' Institute, Venice

Ben Clement
Diploma Architecture (2006)
Tutors: *Elizabeth Dow* and *Jonathan Hill*

The 'Bankrupts' Institute' is derived from the narrative of William Hogarth's *A Rake's Progress* (1733). In the proposal, the lives of the residents – who are recovering bankrupts – productively shape the building through an economy of generosity. The act of giving sustains not only the inhabitants of the institute, continually reshaping its architecture, but also the city around it. The architecture thereby acts as currency in an economy where more traditional currencies, possessions and furniture are left behind. Built components, including a 'Revealing Screen' and a 'Constraining Wall', are all exchangeable elements in the project's symbolic gift economy.

Basilica of San Clemente, Rome

Kenny Tsui
MArch Architecture (2007)
Tutors: *Marjan Colletti* and *Marcos Cruz*

This MArch project entails a chapel extension at the Basilica of San Clemente, a complex of three churches built in different periods one above the other. Apart from the intricacy of post-parametric geometries, various architectural references re-enact a challenging conversation on sacred spaces, religious decorative patterns and figural ornaments. These are constructed within the various historic sediments of the basilica in which ornamented skins and veils articulate a series of embodied voids that seem to exfoliate, breathe and sweat. Overall, the work explores the ornamental density of an inhabitable architectural flesh, where the sumptuousness of its sublime interiors results from a reinterpretation of pre-modern typologies and narratives of spiritual spaces.

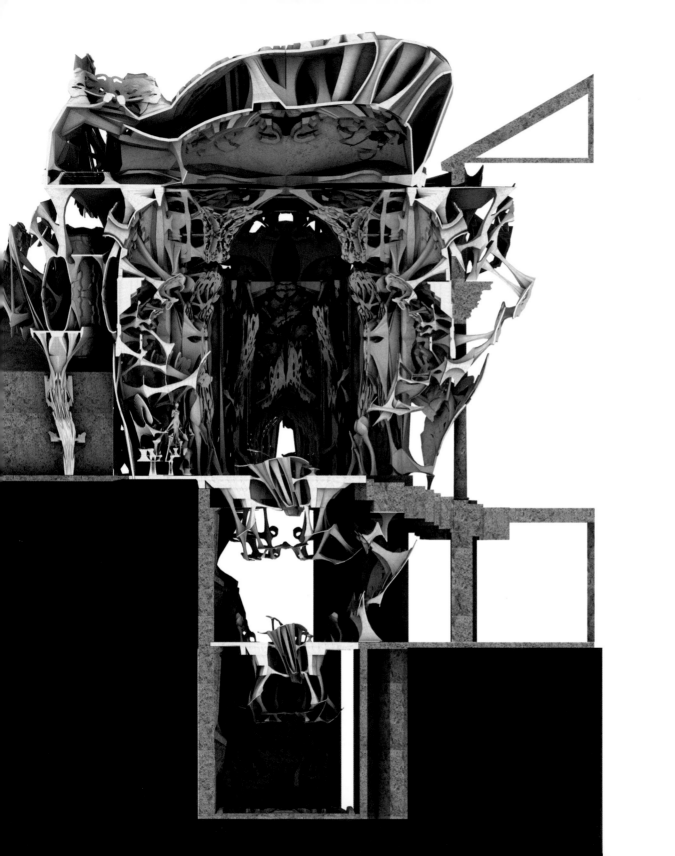

Berlin Infection

Peter Kidger
Diploma Architecture (2006)
Tutors: *Nic Clear* and *Simon Kennedy*

In an empty city, strange forms start to congregate; they move through the deserted streets and begin to assemble themselves. The city is London, and the object that begins to self-construct itself is the iconic Berlin Fernsehturm (television tower). This autopoesis suggests a form of architectural seeding, multivalence and the ubiquity of the city under late capitalism. Created as a movie, the 'Berlin Infection' is an evocative and technically sophisticated film, mixing computer animation and photographic scenes in order to create a highly convincing *mis-en-scène* that blurs the distinction between the actual and the virtual.

Biotechnology of Breakfast

Sacha Leong
MArch Architectural Design (2005)
Tutor: *Simon Herron*

This polemical project focuses on the potential of bioengineering to become ubiquitous and everyday, and is an artful mix of the scientific with the quotidian domestic. It explores a near architectural future where the technologies of biochemistry are as common and unremarkable as making breakfast. Breakfast, after all, is a biotechnological experiment, practised time and time again. Leong creates a lexicon of elements that can function both as breakfast utensils and biotechnical laboratory equipment. The 'Biotechnology of Breakfast' culminates in a full-size installation. It asks: What is unusual anymore? Are we not indistinguishable from the advanced processes we manage to manipulate? What is normal for humanity now? Are we all not biotechnological engineers?

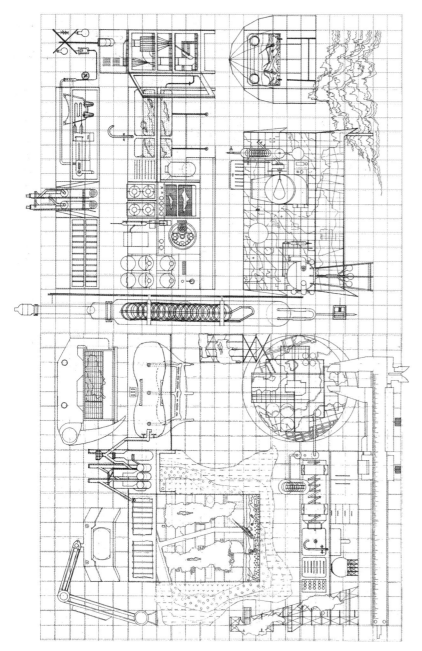

Penelope Haralambidou
PhD Architectural Design (2003)
Supervisor: *Philip Tabor*

The 'Blossoming of Perspective: an Investigation of Spatial Representation' is inspired by Jean-François Lyotard's reading of Marcel Duchamp's secret pornographic assemblage, *Étant donnés: 1° la chute d'eau/2° le gaz d'éclairage* (1946–66), commonly referred to in English as *Given*, as an incarnation, but also inversion, of the rules of linear perspective. Drawing on Duchamp's term 'blossoming' which, in this design-based PhD, is connected with stereoscopy, the thesis analyses *Given* as a physically constructed stereo-drawing. It proposes stereoscopy as the central and intentional theme of *Given*, and stereo-photogrammetry as a creative tool, influencing its intellectual content, guiding its manufacturing process and pointing to an expanded technique of representation in architecture. The work proposes an alternative architectural practice between architectural design, art practice, art history and critical theory, and uses drawing as a critical method.

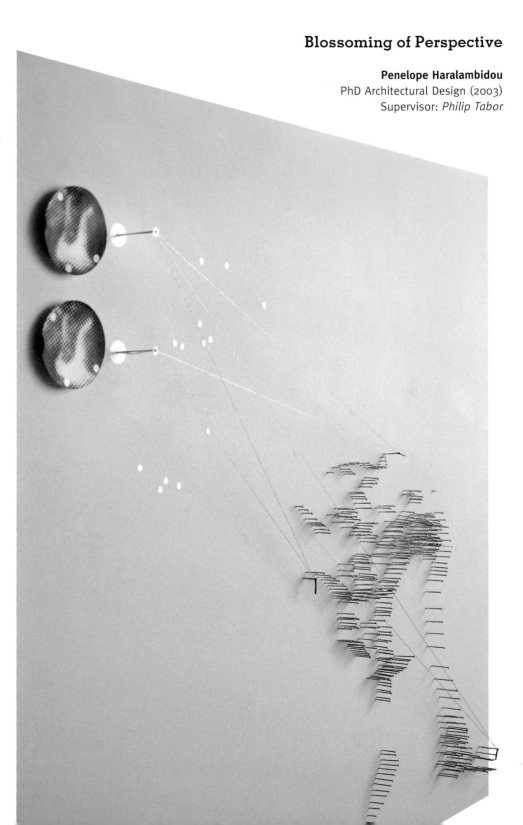

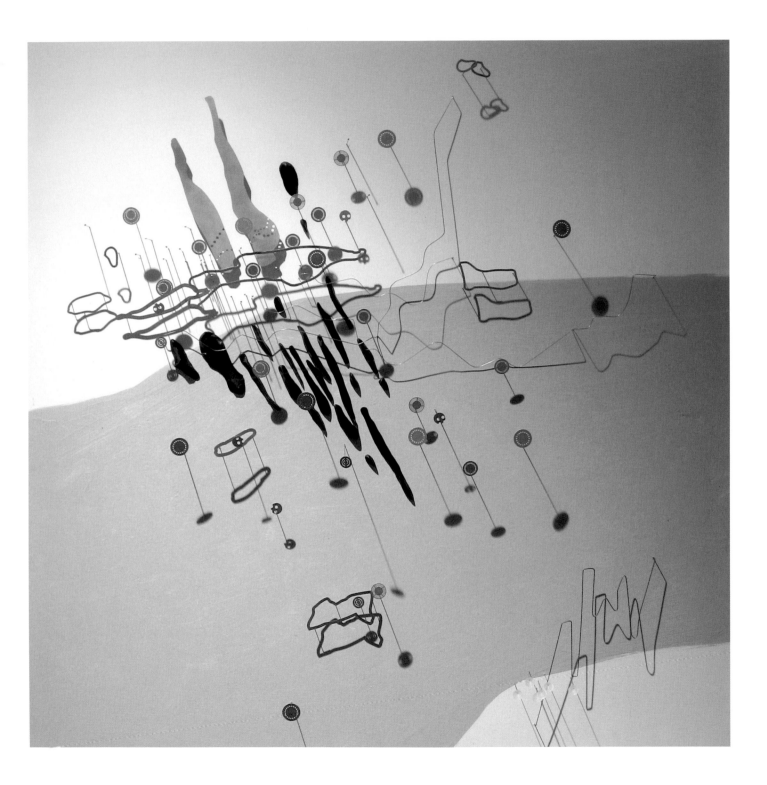

Camden Market Council, London

Dean Pike
Diploma Architecture (2006)
Tutors: *Niall McLaughlin* and *Yeoryia Manolopoulou*

Four administrative chambers enclose a market hall that is used as a micro-government for the market in Camden Town. Using the architectural language of the existing market, a new camouflaged environment made of leather draperies is proposed. Small intimate spaces, nooks and pocket-like rooms weave into the trading operations of the market but contribute to the secrecy of the council. Each space is highly interior, imaginary or dreamlike, and difficult to fathom. 'Unreal' spaces extend as layer-upon-layer is coerced and tailored into walls and rooms. The design is driven by the material investigation of leather and the study of Adolf Loos' concept of *Raumplan*, Joseph Gandy's drawings for John Soane, and wrappings by Christo and Jeanne-Claude.

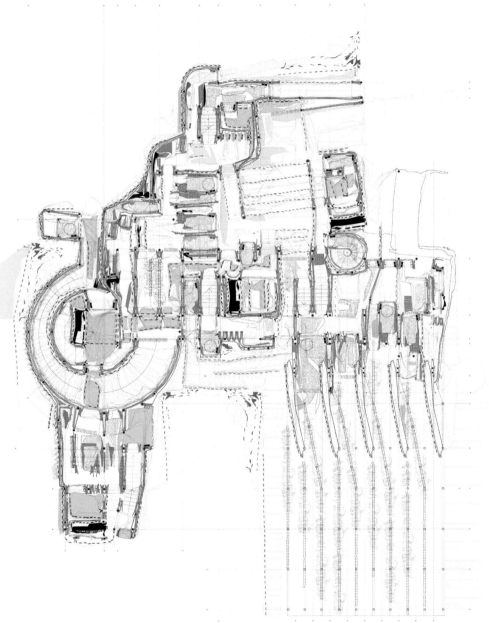

Capacitor, Lea Valley, London

Yumi Saito
Diploma Architecture (2004)
Tutors: *Simon Herron* and *Susanne Isa*

A series of man-powered flying structures populate a group of drifting park landscapes, traversing and grazing the Lea Valley. These lighter-than-air structures are powered by pleasure generated from the work and labour of the users. Helium supported, they are lowered and raised by the capture and release of heat generated from the perspiration of these users. Excess heat is released through the perimeter sweat glands, and the structures encourage delirious speculative play, where the pursuit of pure pleasure is their function. Other elements suspend and drag: free-fall bogies, filigree machines, exoskeletal apparatuses, primary-drive vessels and collaborating assemblies.

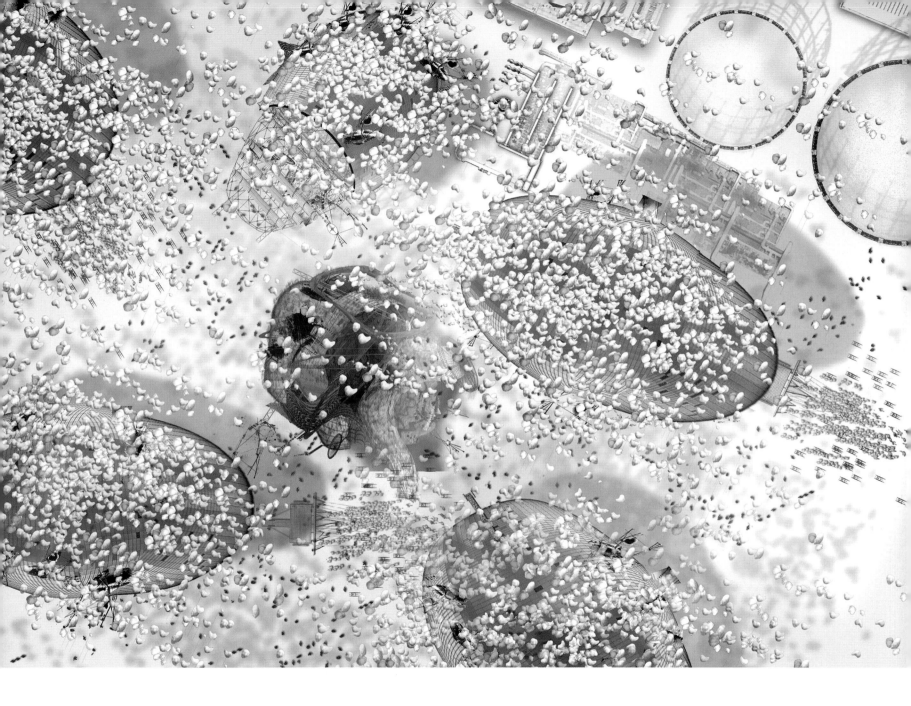

Carbon Casino

Richard Bevan
Diploma Architecture (2008)
Tutors: *Nic Clear* and *Simon Kennedy*

As a response to an imposed carbon tax and to limits on personal carbon allowances, Heathrow Airport opens a new 'Carbon Casino' where high rollers with private jets gamble their carbon allowances – betting against each other and ordinary 'mom and pop' gamblers. The 'house,' as always, takes a cut to sustain its own viability. 'Carbon Casino,' manned by robot card dealers, plays with idea of luxury and decadence all 'paid for' by the carbon credits raised in the casino. Thoroughly researched and worryingly believable. The project is part satire, part polemic, part futuristic fantasy. It eschews the often moralising tendencies of traditional 'environmental' projects and highlights the inherent hypocrisy of a culture that alleviates its responsibilities regarding sustainability. It poses serious questions about the commitment of the architecture industry to deal with its role in certain forms of development.

Casino, Brownsea Island, Poole

Mark Ng
BSc Architecture (2003)
Tutors: *Julia Backhaus* and *Marjan Colletti*

This casino is a mechanically aided, bio-diverse gambling and business park at Brownsea Island, Poole. The veins and blood vessels – the infrastructure of the complex – are ripped out to formally create an artificial jungle for the oriental birds, monkeys and farm animals sourced on site. Just like the live lions at the MGM Grand Hotel in Las Vegas, the wildlife and the hedonistic atmosphere promote vast consumption, whose energy is recycled back into the eco-system, simultaneously and atmospherically: the hot water pipes get warmer, driving those noisy, playful monkeys away, creating a tranquil spot amid the chaos; the left-over food from the casino buffets is redistributed by mechanical buckets, and it's dinner time for the lions! Bird droppings make the soil rich, and the cows reap the rewards – but ultimately, they are gulped back down by the gluttons …

Cathedral and Catacomb for a Cultural Treasure

Kevin Bai
Diploma Architecture (2008)
Tutors: *Simon Herron* and *Susanne Isa*

The protagonist 'K' is a young apprentice architect working for 'N', a leading figure in architecture, without 'K' ever knowing 'N' personally. Everything 'K' understands about 'N' comes from rumours, gossip and his perception of back catalogue projects. 'K' becomes an extension of 'N', effectively his avatar, and struggles to distinguish himself from his hero. This narrative project proposes a quasi-religious scheme for 'N', comprising a memory theatre and catacomb over which stands a cathedral. Following Marcel Duchamp, Kurt Schwitters and Joseph Cornell, who all made art by assembling found objects, 'K' recycles pre-existing building elements designed by 'N', and then reconfigures these elements into the project narrative. In doing so, 'K' conceptualises architecture as new spatial programmes and cultural identities.

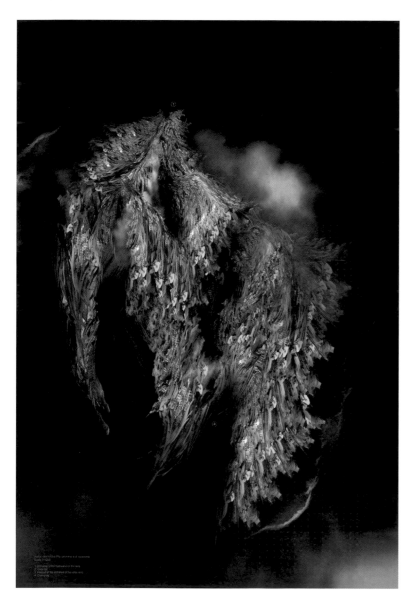

Cinema and Lecture Theatres, Venice

Christopher Wong
BSc Architecture (2008)
Tutors: *Julia Backhaus* and *Pedro Font Alba*

Despite Venice's colourful history of exploration, it has transformed in to an insular city swamped by tourists. Situated on Giudecca, a large residential island just south of Venice's central mass, the project provides a cinema and lecture theatre complex as a forum for social exploration, and so allows locals to escape their introverted environment by exploring exotic cultures. The building is composed of three lecture theatres and a cinema, a library, audio-visual editing suite and a restaurant. Three small apartments accommodate explorers invited to speak at the forum. The building is above ground level in order to maintain two 'scapes': the natural landscape below and the constructed landscape above. The natural landscape acts as a public garden, providing a pleasant social gathering area for locals.

Clothed House

Zoe Quick
Diploma Architecture (2002)
Tutors: *Elizabeth Dow* and *Jonathan Hill*

Countering excessive domestic energy consumption, 'Clothed House' identifies the 1940s as a period when sustainability, recycling and self-help were valued and necessary. With the skill and resourcefulness of the Second World War housewife as a model, 'make do and mend' as a motto, and a willing grandmother as a consultant, Quick conceives domestic insulation as seasonal clothing rather than as permanent building material. Clothing the home the way we clothe the body, architectural 'garments' are worn in layers to form an environmental and ergonomic 'ensemble' specific to each season. Fabricating a new home garment or repairing an old one, the user is active rather than sedentary, reducing energy consumption and encouraging a culture of re-use within the neighbourhood.

Collections of a Mud Lark

Sarah Bromley
BSc Architecture (2007)
Tutors: *Abigail Ashton* and *Andrew Porter*

The architecture of the 'Collections of a Mudlark' project is constructed from detritus that has been dredged from the River Thames in London during varying tidal conditions. A mudlark hoards the pieces he has recovered on a series of piers, these piers being in turn constructed from the found objects. As the piers grow, more detritus can be collected. The site has occasional public access, dependent on the tides, while especially prized possessions are displayed in a series of glass cabinets along the river bank. The project thus responds to environmental concerns with waste and recycling, creating an architecture that both reacts to and exploits these conditions.

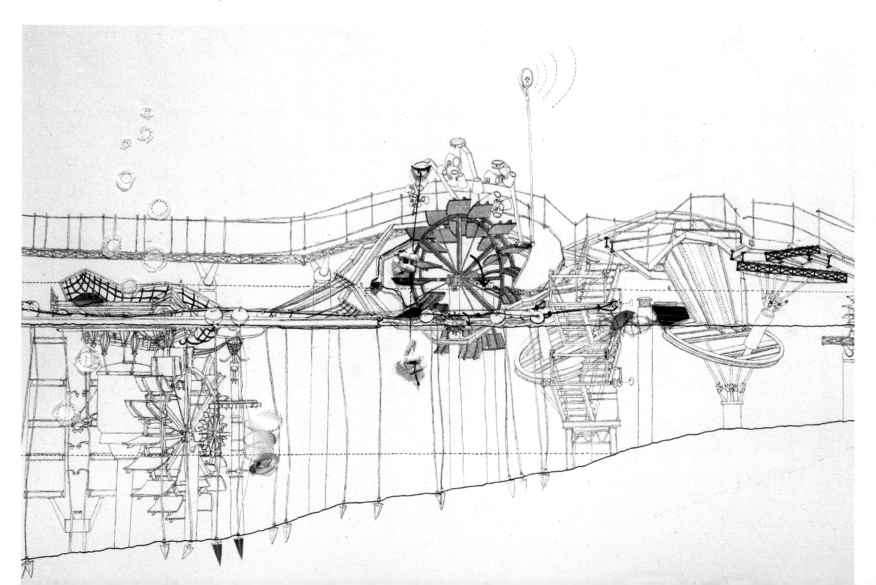

Continua

Neil Spiller, Simon Herron and **Susanne Isa**

This turbulent refusal of the mind to accept the given, ever substituting its own interpretations, has been called by Gaston Bachelard surrationalism. This term indicates the whole state of mind in which the mind is supposedly liberated from the restrictions of logic by its own caprice. Surrationalism traces its origin to Lobatchewsky's discovery of non-Euclidian geometry. For centuries a hardened rationalism has repeated the axioms and postulates of Euclidian geometry, without seeing that they may be freely rejected as they were freely accepted. Lobatchewsky dialecticised geometry and in so doing cast doubt on the fundamental issues, challenging the human mind to rise above them and free itself by its own imprudence.

Charles E. Gauss, *The Aesthetic Theories of French Artists, from Realism to Surrealism*, (1949)

Surrounding the surface of the Earth is an ever growing meta-skin. This skin is a skin of communication, electromagnetic radiation and digital transmission. Every day it drills deeper into our existence. Contemporary architects have no choice but to couch their work within the epistemologies and connectivity of this skin's hyper-links, geo-tags, nested cartography and its hybrid ecologies of cyber fauna and flora. This is a world mostly invisible to us, a world on top of our anthropocentric reality. This is a 'sur' real architectural topology, which slips beyond the merely invisible world of the electromagnetic spectrum to the yet to be seen world of dark matter.

In the contemporary pot-pourri of possible architectural spacescapes, the dogmas and doctrines of old-fashioned white, clean and neat Modernism are redundant. Many fashionable architects have taken these conditions as an excuse to construct highly complex formal exercises with little or no intellectual or pragmatic reason – by contrast, we believe that projects must be innovative, multi-contextual and intellectually sustained. We recognise that a site is a whole series of ecological meta-pathways that stretch far outside a building's legal domain. We believe in the individual, their personal architecture, their exceptional particularity and their ability to create their own spaces constructed by personal logics. It is through designing that we make and understand our world. Our vision of the future is one not dogged by architectural stylistic ubiquity but consists of beautiful, thoughtful difference. In our future, 'rules' are there to broken, projects are multi-layered and are designed by architects and designers who are intrepid explorers. These are our principal protagonists in an experimental architectural laboratory where doing is theory, and less is a bore.

The experience of contemporary architectural designers is one of positioning their work in relation to the following seven continua:

Space – is a continuum of space that stretches from 'treacle' space standing in a field, no computer, no mobile phone, no connectivity whatsoever, to full bodily immersion in cyberspace. Along the way between these two extremes are all manner of mixed and augmented spaces.

Technology – is means, not meaning. Like space, technology ranges from simple prosthetics (the stone axe) via the Victorian cog and cam, to the valve, capacitor, logic gate, the integrated circuit, the central processing unit, the quantum computer, the stem cell, the monocot and a million states and applications between and beyond.

Narrative, Semiotics and Performance – is myth. An architect, designer, explorer can choose whether their work operates along a continuum that ranges from minimal engagement in quotation or mnemonic nuance in relation to the history of culture or the contemporary world, or embraces the multiplicity of the complex and emergent universes of discourse that we inhabit. A design might conjure new conjunctions of semiotics as a way of re-reading them. It also might integrate itself with human and cultural memory, and it might be reflexive and performative (in real time or retrospectively).

Cyborgian Geography – an architect-designer-explorer now can posit work, which operates in all manner of mixed and augmented terrains that are subject to all manner of geomorphic and cybermorphic factors and drivers.

Scopic Regimes – architecture can exist at all scales. It all depends on the resolution of the scope that one chooses to use: continents, oceans, cities, streets, rooms, carpets, micro landscapes and medico landscapes are all part of this continuum of weight and measure.

Sensitivity – an architect-designer-explorer might decide to make objects, spaces or buildings whose parts are sensitive, that pick up environmental variations or receive information. These sensors, therefore, can make objects and buildings that are influenced by events elsewhere, or indeed are influential elsewhere.

Time – is the central ingredient to this heady elixir. All the above six continua can be time dependent. Therefore our new protagonists, architects, designers and explorers can 'mix' the movement of their spaces, buildings and objects up and down the other six continua. So a design might oscillate the spaces within itself with varying elements of vitality over time. A design might use different technologies at different times in its existence. A design might perform complex mnemonic tableaux at certain points in its life cycle. A design might demand of its occupants the use of a different lens with which to see other than anthropocentric phenomena or spaces. A design might coerce the occupant to be aware of environmental conditions in other locations that change. A design might change the sensitivity of objects over time, dulling them sometimes, making them hypersensitive at other times.

Many of the projects in this book operate spatial fields that are numerous, complex and susceptible to chance and change. These include ideas about how to: re-boot torn natural ecologies with artificial catalytic ones; how we might harness the growth imperative of plants and be able to grow some of our products in a clean and sustainable way; how we might create 21st-century memorials and other mnemonic spaces; how we might tell stories to bring the power of our architecture alive; how we might create locative and performing architecture; and how we might embroider space at micro and macro scales. Such projects can take as initial points of departure ideas from the history of art, or the history of ideas or even from the history of architecture. But all projects shown here are conscious of the role in the continuity of radical architectural thought that goes back via Philip Webb, Claude-Nicolas Ledoux and Plato's Cave. We make marks in the future and carve out territories for further exploration.

Points of view cascade, epistemologies are anamorphically distorted to reveal architectures that prove that surrealism invigorated by advanced technology is a useful paradigm for architects to research in the early 21st century. Marvel and enjoy this work, take it for what it is: sublime vignettes of a world that is already here.

Cortical Plasticity

Dan Farmer
Diploma Architecture (2008)
Tutors: *Nic Clear* and *Simon Kennedy*

'Cortical Plasticity' refers to the changes that occur in the organisation of the brain as a result of experience. It is possible for brain activity associated with a given function to move to a different location as a consequence of brain damage or recovery. As a response to a particular condition, the neuronal circuits within the visual cortex may undertake a detailed level cortical and sub-cortical re-wiring. Consequently, perception is altered, including the construction of architectural spaces and physicality of objects that occupy these new environments.

This would suggest that the creation of an architectural space is directly encoded into the neuronal circuits of the brain. The project explores other worlds that might be opened if the physiology of the brain became the site of a speculative architecture. Incorporating technically sophisticated post-production techniques, it truly creates a world where the gap between virtual and actual is meaningless.

Cosmic House, Trafalgar Square, London

Tim Norman
Diploma Architecture (2008)
Tutors: *Neil Spiller* and *Phil Watson*

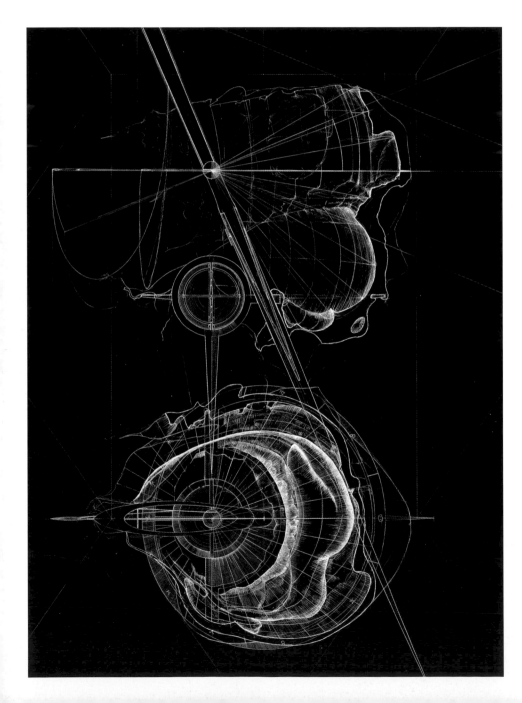

'Cosmic House' is a *magnum opus*; it evolves from the concept of a miniature solar system positioned above the centre of London. The project tracks Venus and explores orbits, collisions and alignments. It builds a universe of discourse that touches on optics, relativity, mythology, symbolism and history; architectural pieces are actors in a time-based spatial symphony – an architectural cosmology.

Norman uses anamorphosis as a method to navigate this collapsed solar system. As he writes in his thesis: 'Listen! the Solar System has come unstuck in Time, Venus reclines nonchalantly in the National Gallery, people gawk at her every day, Saturn is a grapefruit, its pips orbit its citrusian satellites, Jupiter parades through Buckingham Palace … the Thames, like all great rivers of the world, is a Milky Way.'

Culture

Ben Campkin and **cj Lim**

At the beginning of the 21st century, the concept 'culture' and the adjective 'cultural' occupy uneasy territories. On the one hand, they are so rich, nuanced and embedded in everyday language that we can hardly avoid them. On the other hand, they have become so complicated and multi-layered that they inhabit a linguistic minefield. Anxieties about 'culture' as a concept are not new. In 1976, the pioneer of cultural studies, Raymond Williams, wrote in his seminal book *Keywords: a Vocabulary of Culture and Society* that '[c]ulture is one of the two or three most complicated words in the English language', and noted that its significance was in the wide-range and promiscuous relations between its different referents. Only a few years after writing his entry in *Keywords*, however, Williams himself famously declared that he wished he had 'never heard of the damned word'.[1]

Williams cautions us that culture is so complex that the concept is best defined in relation to specific disciplines. Architecture did not make it into his book, although it is embraced by the broad definition of culture as 'the works and practices of intellectual and especially artistic activity'.[2] What new relationships are emerging between architecture and culture at the beginning of the 21st century? How is architecture involved in culture's definition, and vice versa? What happens when the two terms – architecture and culture – are conceived as being conjoined? How are ideas of culture, or more appropriately, cultures, being creatively scrutinised and redefined through the inventions of contemporary architectural design?

Many of the projects included in this collection suggest different configurations of architecture and culture as they relate to: contemporary conditions and current debates, novel modes of architectural practice and technologies, and innovations in forms of representation. Culture is approached by Bartlett architecture students from a plethora of surprising perspectives, in ambitious, original and rigorous ways. Because students come from a broad diversity of backgrounds they can reflect on, and elucidate, the full range of meanings associated with this concept, as articulated by Williams and other scholars of culture: from its origins in natural cultivation, to the pursuit of intellectual development, to grand collective processes of civilisation. En route we encounter the counter-cultural, the subcultural and the irreverent street slang 'culchah' – protests at different forms of cultural domination.

The selected work also represents the full range of geographical scales: from meditations on the fluid nature of individual subjective identity; to reflections on collective value systems; global travel and transportation; cultural displacement, imperialism and colonisation; regional and national identity; transculturation and international relations. From China to Britain, Luxor to Tokyo, Macau to 'Oz', visions of future worlds prompt us to revise conceptions of the dynamics between the local and the global, the near and the far. Practices, artefacts and other phenomena which define particular places and peoples are transposed to new and unexpected contexts, often by students from overseas who, while working in Britain, are absorbing the nutrients of a 'foreign soil'. In the process, individual cultural values are tried, tested and re-evaluated through reflections on personal identity.

Similarly, through the technologies and materials they employ, and the narratives they develop, a number of the featured projects construct new understandings of relationships between nature and culture, in diverse urban, suburban and rural contexts. These schemes return us to the etymological origins of culture in 'cultivation', and provide insights through which urban understandings of nature might be rethought.

On a social level, many of the projects included in this anthology challenge preconceptions about 'high' and 'low', 'elite' and 'popular', 'official' and 'street' culture. Through designs and texts, they demonstrate some of the ways that architecture is bound up with the production of what sociologist Pierre Bourdieu refers to as 'cultural capital', or with the construction of distinctions between different cultural forms. Some projects articulate protest at the hegemony of particular cultural values and processes, others explore and question specific customs and traditions of particular peoples, while others still place emphasis on forgotten or marginal 'sub-cultures', or on the gendering or class-based nature of cultural systems. Such concerns, which have featured strongly in academic debates since Williams was writing in the 1970s, have been extended, re-shaped and brought into alignment with present-day issues.

In a contemporary context, one of the most poignant conceptions of culture referred to by Williams is that of the English philosopher and statesman Francis Bacon (1561–1626), who defined culture as the 'manurance of minds' – that is, both as the improvement of minds and as the growing and cultivation of minds. This metaphor, which conflates the natural and civil definitions of culture outlined by Williams, succinctly connects numerous projects in this book which are fertile with new thinking on the subject. Overall, these students' investigations reinforce an understanding of culture as a process that, on numerous levels, is inherently architectural, and, even in an age dominated by globalisation and global culture,[3] is bound to specific spatial and material contexts.

References
1 Raymond Williams, *Keywords: a Vocabulary of Culture and Society*, Croom Helm Ltd (London), 1976; Tony Bennett, Lawrence Grossberg and Meaghan Morris (eds), *New Keywords: a Revised Vocabulary of Culture and Society*, Blackwell (Oxford), 2005, p 63.
2 Williams, *Keywords*, p 80.
3 Anthony D King, *Spaces of Global Cultures: Architecture, Urbanism, Identity*, Routledge (London), 2004, p 26.

Death Academy

James Hampton
Diploma Architecture (2006)
Tutors: *Elizabeth Dow* and *Jonathan Hill*

Sited on the edge of Campo Santa Maria dei Miracoli in Venice, and taking its narrative from Seneca's *On the Shortness of Life*, James Hampton's 'Accademia della Morte' (Death Academy) seeks to encourage a more public discourse on death, aiding private reflection. The building is part academy, part hospice and part memorial. Exploiting the energy and ambiguity of a building site, the 'Accademia della Morte' is simultaneously under construction and in ruin. To evoke memories of past lives, its architecture draws on the traditional timber carving methods of the Lombardo family who constructed the church in the square of the same name.

Marjan Colletti
PhD Architectural Design (2007)
Supervisor: *Jonathan Hill*

'Digital Poetics' (subtitled 'an Enquiry into the Properties of "Mimetic Intrafaces" and the "Twoandahalf Dimensionality" of Computer-Aided Architectural Design') bridges the gap between architectural theory and the built environment. The PhD thesis criticises pure parametric and algorithmic computerised architecture in favour of a poetic digital avant-garde, equally developed through three-dimensional software and Computer Numerically Controlled (CNC), Rapid Prototyping (RP), and Computer-Aided Design and Computer-Aided Manufacturing (CAD/CAM) technologies. The proposition explores how to combine (analogue) parameters and (digital) properties, hypothesising the concept of 'mimetic intraface' as merger, and the vectorial twoandahalf dimensionality of CAD. Colletti contends that, due to its narrative potential, 'original digitality' should be defined and fashioned both in design and in text.

Throughout the thesis, the concept of 'volution' is adopted to provide an ontological and phenomenological enquiry into a designer-digitality interaction and feedback system. Multiple viewpoints of observation are proposed in order to reveal, or at least approach, 'Digital Poetics'.

SURFACES AND BLOBS-BOUNDARIES IN FACT RENDERED BOUNDARIES ARE NOTHING BUT FLAT.

Dog Racing Track, Baku

Rhys Cannon
Diploma Architecture (2004)
Tutors: *Peter Hasdell* and *Patrick Weber*

The site of Baku's ex-parade ground – Freedom Square – plays host to two conditions. First, a greyhound racing track forms its centrepiece and a lack of bureaucracy, environmentalists and moralistic taboos enables the darkest of blood sports to be performed in the depths of the Palace of Dogs. Second, Azerbaijan relies heavily on the continuing investment of multi-national companies in the offshore oilfields of the Caspian Sea, and in the onshore refinery operations and pipelines.

The track is the centre of an intense gambling arena; the race results and dog 'form' reflect the performance of stocks and shares on the world market. A responsive facade to the existing and partially derelict Absheron Hotel acts as track and trading-floor 'totaliser' (a physical board or electronic ticker instantly displaying the current race or market data). The building thus forms a giant totaliser, reflecting the link between the two gambling models, and enhancing the betting experience of the individuals at the track.

Doing Un-doing Over-doing Re-doing

Sophie Handler
MA Architectural History (2004)
Supervisor: *Jane Rendell*

In this masters dissertation, two stories deploy the symbolic and spatial fabrications of lace as a way of unravelling and rewriting the discipline and object of architectural narrative. Written between the textile archives of Nottingham and the heavily lace-furnished interior of an iconic modernist home in Moscow, in 'Doing Un-doing Over-doing Re-doing' these two alternative stories of creation and construction are built up through the residual details of the furnished home (of lace curtains, antimacassars, cloth panels).

From the symbolic production of a confined and regulated femininity indoors, to the subversive de-construction of a modernist home through its over-decorated interior, these samples of lace cloth become the critical accessories for producing an alternative account of a less visible form of architectural production. Moving away from flattened-out descriptions of inhabitation as a limiting practice of two dimensions – of surface creation and ornamentation – these stories make use of the residual objects of the home-furnished interior as objects for an alternative construction of three dimensions, where decoration operates as an active work of spatial production (layering over, filling and furnishing, subverting, unravelling and reshaping internal space). The theoretical re-centering of this 'textilic' accessory within a more solid structural discipline of 'proper' architectural building prioritises the ordinary, the inferior and less visible – the familiar motifs of domesticity and femininity. The leftover objects of an inhabited interior become the textilic strategy for re-writing the subject and object of standard architectural production.

Domestic Sedimentary Space

Lisa Silver
Diploma Architecture (2002)
Tutors: *Salvador Perez Arroyo* and *Marcos Cruz*

In the heart of Mississippi County, near the small town of Greenville, three characters are confined to three rooms within a house. The initial part of the project narrates a psychological response to imprisonment within these rooms, whereby, in order to survive, the characters collect mundane objects to create a more stimulating living space. In the second part of the project, the characters gradually transform the house from inside out, colonising the site in the form of an enclave, which combines living with object-based enterprises that illustrate their particular idiosyncrasies. The garage becomes a car mechanic's workshop; the study room provides space for research and archiving; and the bathroom transforms into a voyeuristic viewing point on the site.

Drawing On Chance

Yeoryia Manolopoulou
PhD Architectural Design (2003)
Supervisor: *Philip Tabor*

This PhD design-based thesis – 'Drawing On Chance: Indeterminacy, Perception and Design' – argues that architecture is a product and a producer of both design and chance. Architecture influences our perceptual and aesthetic habits while our habits, in turn, tend to bound the limits of architectural language in a continuous circle. An accident may help us break out of this impasse: chance events may upset the routines of perception to stimulate imagination.

The thesis asks: Could chance itself be explored as a design tool, and how could this affect the ways in which space is represented, produced and occupied? The argument is built on the investigation of art projects, particularly Marcel Duchamp's *The Bride Stripped Bare by Her Bachelors, Even,* (1915 – 23), and the production of Manolopoulou's own design work. It suggests the formulation of chance as a drawing apparatus for cultivating indeterminacy and defines the techniques of 'impulsive', 'active' and 'measurable' chance. The conclusion proposes that the mechanisms of chance may drive architecture to a non-optical account of space.

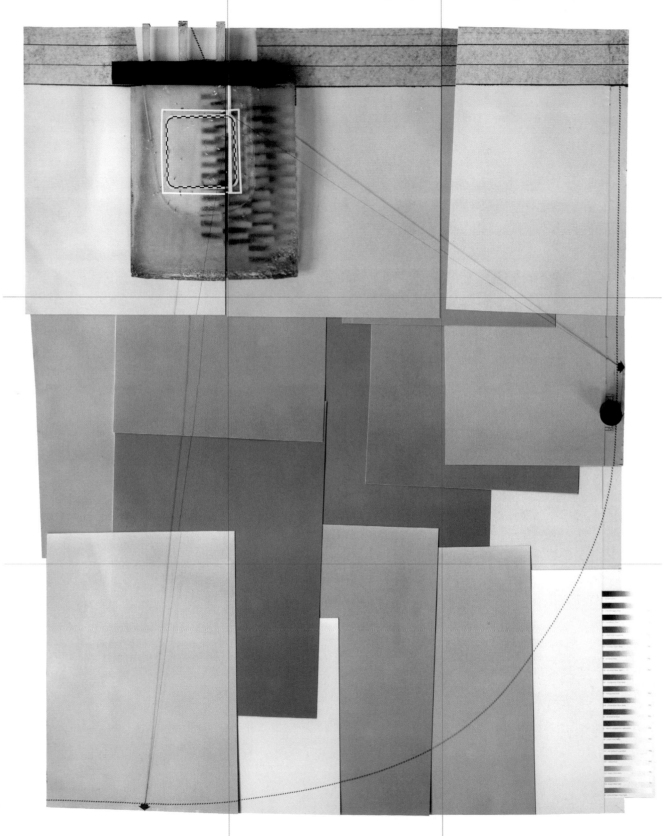

Dreaming of Flight

Tristan Wigfall
Diploma Architecture (2007)
Tutors: *John Puttick* and *Peter Szczepaniak*

Trellick Tower is an iconic piece of Brutalist architecture designed by the Hungarian emigré architect Ernö Goldfinger, and completed in 1972. Standing some 31 storeys tall, and boasting a semi-disengaged lift tower, it offers a strangely brooding presence in London's north-west landscape. In this project's narrative, a man is locked in the uppermost plant room. With no other means of escape, he decides to learn to fly, which he attempts to do by capturing and dissecting local pigeons who make the mistake of coming too close. The final installation of this project shows a particular moment in time, the man has fully digested his birdly lessons, and has just taken flight out of a window. Whether he has succeeded or not is unknown.

Efflorescent Drawing Device

Ryan Martin
Diploma Architecture (2007)
Tutors: *Bob Sheil* and *Graeme Williamson*

Through the exploration, detection and exploitation of materials and micro-environmental phenomena within a medieval crypt, this project readorns internal surfaces with visio-decorative illuminations. It draws upon historical data, scientific theory, art theory and memory to distil a set of visual and atmospheric criteria that inform the simulated reillumination of medieval space.

In 2004, at the medieval church of St Olave's in London, a precarious lime tree had to be removed from the courtyard. As a consequence, efflorescence that had been kept at bay for decades gradually overcame the crypt's vaults. Imagining the crypt's original decoration, Martin's non-intrusive instruments scrape the vaulted ceiling of salts at an imperceptible pace to the eye. Salt residue is then channelled through a series of glass pipettes and deposited on the crypt floor as new 'projected frescos'. The project suggests that intimate understanding of the physical and tactile is central to the holistic scope of the designer's imagination.

Elements, Kai Tak City

Jan Kattein
Diploma Architecture (2002)
Tutors: *Elizabeth Dow* and *Jonathan Hill*

Housing the former residents of the Walled City of Kowloon, the urban elements proposed by this project are sited within the disused Kai Tak Airport. These elements are designed and constructed as responses to the cultural and social history of the city's residents. Electricity for street lighting is generated by a series of wobbly bridges that link the former runway with the centre of Kowloon. The new city centre is marked by a wooden shrine, which travels up and down a 10-metre steel tower, powered by the wind caught in a bamboo and silk propeller. Its movement is extremely slow, allowing the growing city time to evolve and adapt.

Emperor's Castle, Tokyo

Thomas Hillier
Diploma Architecture (2008)
Tutors: *Bernd Felsinger* and *cj Lim*

A woodblock landscape by Japanese *ukiyo-e* printmaker Ando Hiroshige, inspired Hillier to replace Hiroshige's characters in this project with architectonic metaphors set within Tokyo's Imperial Palace. The Princess, a flexible diaphanous membrane, frantically knits herself in the hope of reaching the grass perimeter of the Cowherd, only to be prevented by the Emperor, represented by a collection of breathing origami lungs. The Emperor's army, using a complex pulley system, demands that the knitting begins again and again and articulates the manipulations. Here, architecture employs narrative to examine current cultural and social issues in Japan: unconditional piety, a relentless work ethic and conservative attitudes of love.

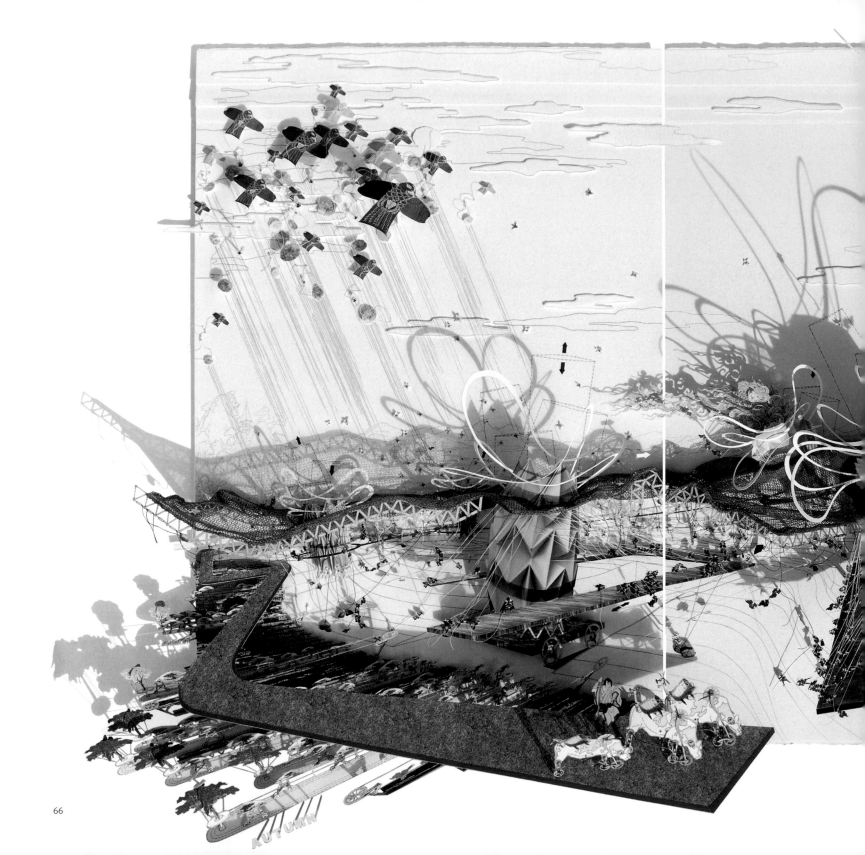

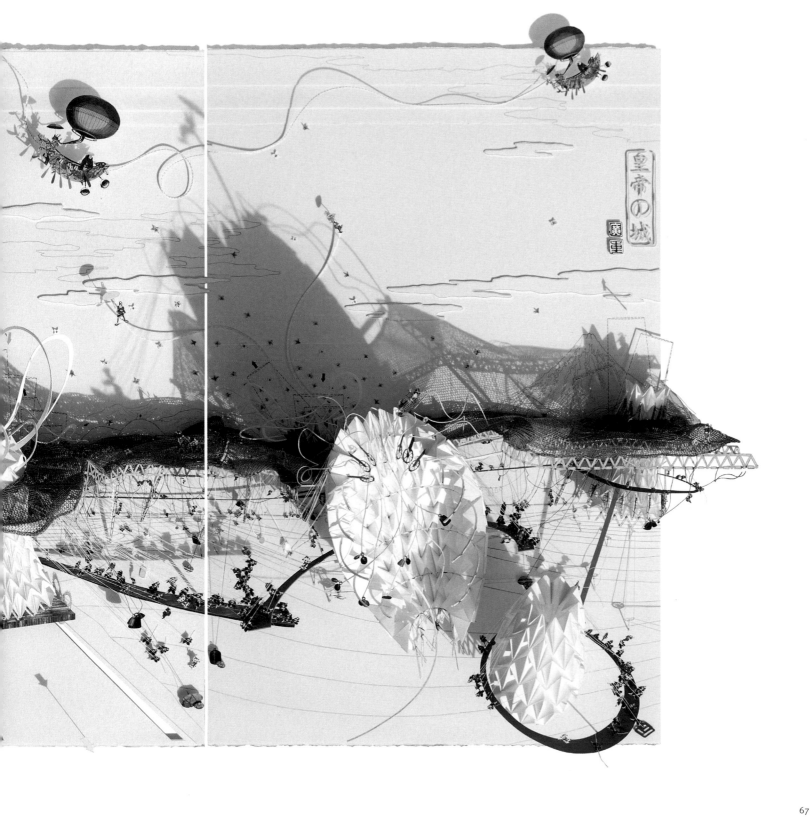

English Tropical Garden, Isles of Scilly

Thomas Dunn
Diploma Architecture (2008)
Tutors: *Bob Sheil* and *Emmanuel Vercruysse*

A mechanical garden, constructed as indigenous architecture, is set within the Tropical Gardens of Tresco on the Scilly Isles, facing into the Gulf Stream. This is an imaginary future environment in extreme flux, where elements of the existing landscape are tended by a flock of 'evolutionary machines' that gather soil, seed, moisture and light to sustain the garden's history of alien cultivation. The project involved research into existing archaeological records in order to reveal diverse and indigenous forces that inform the design proposal, including environmental and meteorological data, cultural events, mythologies and local histories. Speculative and intuitive ideas are reviewed in the context of selected architectural, artistic, historical and environmental theories.

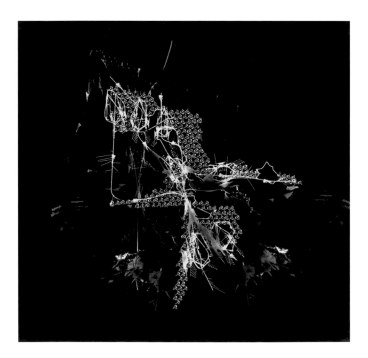

Environmental Parasite, London

Jacobus Strauss
Diploma Architecture (2007)
Tutors: *David Ardill* and *Colin Fournier*

The environmental parasite, or 'Mosquito', is a pod that attaches itself to existing buildings. It appears to be a robotic insect making its way up its host's exterior. Basic survival systems plug into the infrastructure of the host, tapping into its water, power, waste management and communications technology. This makes the relationship parasitic. However, the parasite can feed its own inputs back to the host: the wings are solar panels that also collect rainwater on their large surface area, resulting in mutual benefits for both parties. The pod can move on, leaving behind only a little sting where it had implanted small bolts to attach itself to the host.

Fabrication

Bob Sheil, Mark Smout and Marjan Colletti

It is difficult to find a single design project at the UCL Bartlett School of Architecture that, at some point or another, has not been altered or initiated by an expedition into the physical and tactile attributes of architecture. It is equally difficult to find a graduate who, at one time or another, has not spent days or weeks in the Bartlett's workshops, or in the studio or at home, piecing, chopping, sewing, pouring, joining, capturing or reinventing their ideas through intuitive or calculated experimentation. Whether you attend the annual Summer Show, one of the innumerable reviews, or are just passing through the Bartlett, the chances are you will be faced with an abundance of curiously made artefacts and constructs. But just what are you looking at, in this outpouring of all manner of fabrication? Are they models, props, fragments, full-scale prototypes, immersive environments or simply drawings without paper? Are they analogous assemblies, exploring ephemeral or non-tangible ideas? Are they design tools or designs in themselves? Are they substitutes for expression that is unspeakable? Just what are they scrutinising, and what are they seeking to explore that advanced virtual representation cannot achieve more rapidly (and, in most cases, via less arduous methods)? Questions such as these are met by vigorous debate among the diverse groups that constitute the Bartlett's intense atmosphere of architectural discourse.

There are those who see no separation between drawing, model, or building, as either verbs or nouns, treating them as potential to invent and hypothesise design propositions. They adopt a 'by any means appropriate' approach towards the practice of design, where design is a haptic experience in which the physical act of piecing ideas together presents and represents the very matter of the problem. Here, 'modelling' is adopted as a reflective or systematic tool to follow or assist predictions. Scrutiny leads to serendipity, and crafted drawings sit alongside, or even within, iridescent models where the essence of architectural intent is transmitted through the persuasive and seductive visions of the designer's eye and hand. Inventive and intuitive speculation of this kind is exercised through the power of representation as a tool to speculate upon the making of architecture and architectural concepts. This approach presents us with the process of design as an instigator and montage of strategies rather than through a narrow focus on any single technique or doctrine.

In other parts of the Bartlett you will hear and witness proclamations that the position of the designer has taken a shift so radical as to rock conventional claims on the origin and direction of architectural discipline. Here, what we might even call 'Neo-Medievalists' are exhuming the tacit traditions of conversation, collaboration, trade and craftsmanship as core architectural disciplines. Theirs is a practice which asserts that how we design has become of equal significance to what we design, raising difficult questions on the traditions of design expertise. Far from regressive in their disposition towards technology, the N-Ms have come into existence through the age of digital fabrication, where making as an experimental design process has returned from the periphery. They argue that what transpires on the workbench, studio desk or kitchen drainer has the capacity to transgress into industrial production. Design, they argue, has become a direct feed to the choreography of manufacturing protocols, and soon N-Ms will have remastered all roles and skills from idea to building. In a new Neo-Medieval Age, design becomes a digital template from which the built artefact is copied. The N-M designer is maker, and thus grasps the opportunity to extend the iterative traditions of representation into modes of prototyping customised architectures.

Another view on making architecture in the wake of evolving tools is to adapt their implicit capabilities as generators to challenge the morphology of architectural disciplines. Here, extraordinary architectures are incubated like liquid specimens from a laboratory Petri dish. These chemists of architecture declare they have overcome the alienation and otherness of virtuality, they have mastered the elegance and intricacy of digital capabilities, and they are pioneering a new hybrid discipline of analogue and digital research generating extraordinary spatial, tectonic and contextual sophistication. The chemists within this book thus propagate a generative strand of strange and familiar character. Opposing the predictive, reductive and impotent obsessions of parametric modelling, theirs is a viral architecture born of fluidity, mutation, ornamentation, ritual and cult. It is an architecture that seeks out the intimate and is contextualised beyond the generic, the global, the ecumenical and the obvious. It is beyond the mechanistic constraints of techniques, technologies and technics. It is convoluted and neoplasmatic.

Elsewhere on the platform of making speculative architecture are those who are focused on constructing prototypes for time-based realities. Their signature is the bleep and hum of ever more curious and magical assemblies, seeking to activate and define new roles for the user and new territories within their environment. Work from these activists operates at the scale of the body, where the audience becomes an inseparable extension of site, subject, materiality, field, performance, feedback and carrier of architectural sensation. Inherent to this world is a curiosity for intricate and bespoke fabrication, sourcing and hacking components, knitting electronics, funnelling data, computational language, as well as for the endless vagaries of environmental and human behaviour. Luring the user in to a neighbourhood of prosthetic, responsive and passive assemblies, the makers of speculative and evolutionary architectural environments dissolve the hard and static boundaries of architecture as a merely formal artefact to a state of real and virtual liquidity.

Upon these polemical diversities, a chorus of gadgets, tools and machinery sound out the daily union of head, hand, heart, material and process. Bartlett air is thus saturated with a complex scent of ideas under manufacture. Some pockets smell of zp®140 dust burning off monitor shells and polymers being sintered by laser, others exude a faint whiff of adhesives bonding, solder fusing and embers charring. Other, well-worn pockets diffuse the pungent aroma of molten metal, timber shavings and tobacco leaf. The subsequent discharge of flotsam and jetsam excretes a fertile landscape of remnants and offcuts, of things familiar and deeply curious, each tracing the expedition path of those who leave it behind and move on. As the debris is finally gathered and removed, Bartlett air is laden with a pungent atmosphere of frenzied resolution as final iterations are refined, translated and, ultimately, magnificently and abundantly released.

Fish Farm, Camargue

Massimo Minale
Diploma Architecture (2004)
Tutors: *Neil Spiller* and *Phil Watson*

Since the Industrial Revolution, bulk-manufacturing processes have polluted and torn apart the delicate interrelationships of the natural world. Those natural relationships set in particular landscapes, geomorphic and economic conditions can create local rituals, cuisine and indigenous variations of animals and plants.

Minale's project is situated in the French Camargue and aims to optimise the indigenous fish population. This is done by using four differently scaled sonic devices, each type being used in varying clusters to guide fish to various aquatic environments that suit the different stages of their particular life cycle – all within the water bodies of the Camargue. The project has diurnal, seasonal and yearly cycles.

The design is informed by Minale's earlier research into micro sound. Under the skin of the musical note lies the realm of micro sound, of sound particles lasting less than a 10th of a second. Recent technological advances allow us to probe and manipulate these pinpoints of sound, dissolving the traditional building blocks of both music and, more importantly, architecture into a more fluid and supple medium.

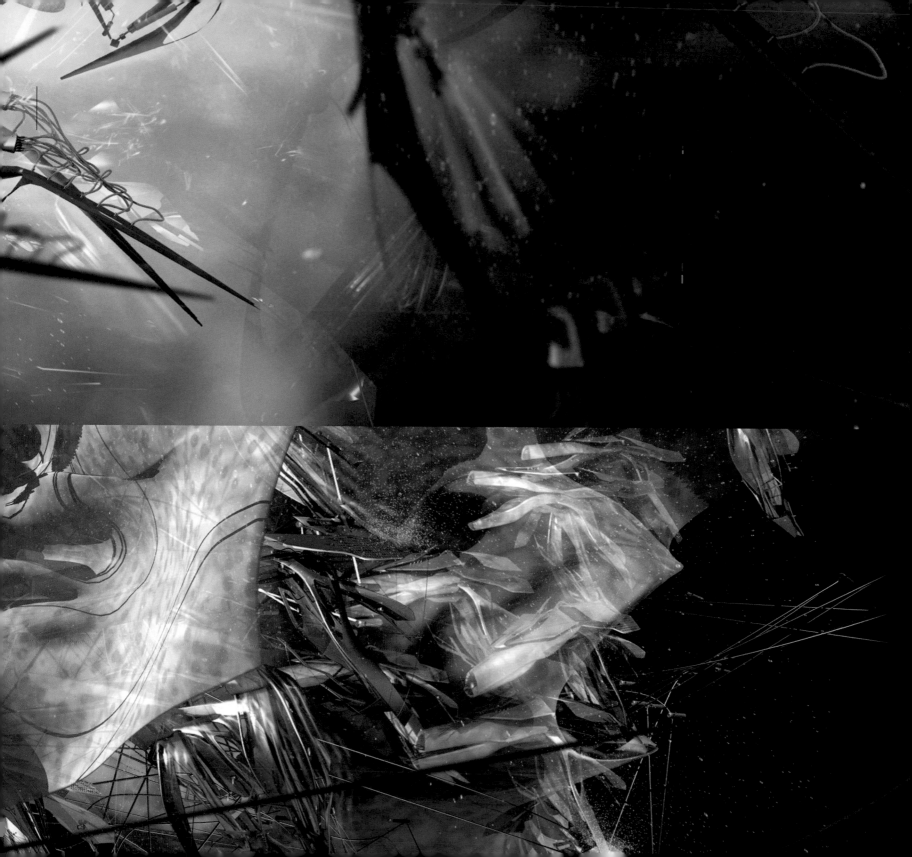

Floating City 2030

Anthony Lau
MArch Architecture (2007)
Tutor: *Colin Fournier*

'Floating City 2030' recognises that rising sea levels threaten coastal cities around the world, and that the future of human habitation may well be to live on water. In this project, the Thames Estuary is the site for aquatic urban expansion as a radical alternative to the prevalent practice of building on flood plains. Every year, hundreds of decommissioned ships and oil platforms are scrapped, and this proposal aims to give them a new lease of life. Reconfigurable floating communities and offshore farms are interconnected by water-based infrastructure and transport systems. Oil platforms form new high-rise developments powered by wind turbines and wave power generators.

Flood House, Rhine Delta

Matthew Butcher
Diploma Architecture (2004)
Tutors: *Elizabeth Dow* and *Jonathan Hill*

Housing the Dutch environment minister and ministry, the 'Flood House' is a prototype for living in, and working with, a seasonally flooded landscape. It has three typologies, each at a different scale; a series of locks control the seasonal disposition of building fragments and sediment banks. Historically, the Dutch lock the land from the sea and inside from outside. The 'Flood House' subverts this tradition. Each lock is a barometer, measuring climatic changes and triggering an appropriate response. Analogous to the environment it inhabits, the 'Flood House' records, responds and reconfigures according to tides, seasons and uses. The house floods and the flood houses.

Flotsam and Jetsam

Michael Garnett
Diploma Architecture (2007)
Tutors: *Bob Sheil* and *Graeme Williamson*

The 'Flotsam and Jetsam' projects are a series of jewellery-like mechanisms for London's wasteland. The projects focus on a large construction site where a number of Black Redstarts live. These are a protected bird species with a strong attraction to cement works, refuse tips, construction debris and decaying structures. As the bird is a rare and protected species, exclusion zones are quickly enforced around the nests of mating pairs, thus causing considerable disruption to building and infrastructure construction. Garnett's machines operate as early warning devices and lures to influence the potential location of the Redstarts' chosen nesting sites and to record the changing environmental influences that act upon them.

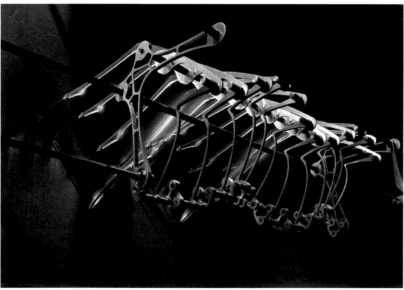

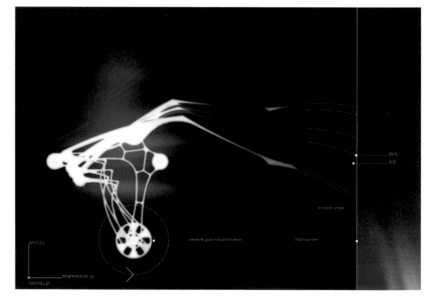

Funerary Landscape

Asif Khan
BSc Architecture (2004)
Tutors: *Laura Allen* and *Mark Smout*

A crematorium for the king and the residents of Oslo is proposed at King Harald's farm on the peninsula of Bygdøy. Upon a vast porcelain landscape constructed over fifty years, seven chapels are built to provide for the needs of seven fictitious funerals: The Baby, The Infant, The Man, The Immigrant, The Matriarch, The Pauper and The King. The programme reconciles a reinterpretation of traditional Viking funeral methods with various subversions of the contemporary. Six distinct materials navigate mourners and their deceased from their sea arrival through precise processional routes. Along these routes, the materials form skins which eventually laminate to form chapels and banqueting halls. After the ceremony, the funeral party ascends on to a porcelain landscape, the translucent fragility of which becomes a symbol for the delicate boundary between two worlds.

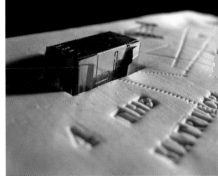

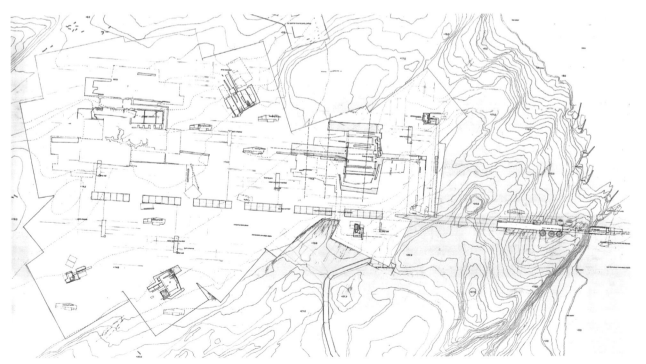

Global Warming Causes Frozen Music to Melt

Bethany Wells
BSc Architecture (2007)
Tutor: *Ben Campkin*

To increase our knowledge we no longer go out on an exploration, but gather the world around us from our seat. The British Library bookmark in front of me claims to offer 'The World's Knowledge', complete with online access to the entire library catalogue: 'Expand your Mind: Shrink the World'.

With the enclosing of the world through technology, the air is our principal means of communication, the invisible lightness of our reaching around the globe. We exist in a post-industrial enchantment with ideas simply held in the air. We can gather anything around us, with technology as our courier. Today the air holds no direction, but all our data.

Where early Modernism rejoiced in a collective seizing and moving of matter through air, as the momentum of the city grew with the rhythm of moving vehicles and moving machinery, today, in post-industrial society, we see a collective seizing and moving of air itself. The commodification, conditioning and directing of air has become an almost obsessive pursuit. It takes up a great deal of our energy, both literally and mentally. This can be seen as a further evolution of 'the intimate unity of the modern self and the modern environment',[1] rendering technology ever more inseparable from the experience of our immediate space:

Click. The windows above in the reading room have just started opening. I can hear the motors. But I can't see the windows. Actually I can't tell whether it's dark outside or not, it's too warm so a slight breeze is let in. It is always bright enough, so it doesn't concern me what the time is.

A perfectly controlled environment (outside of my control).

Today, an increasingly large amount of each building's budget is taken up with the filtering, conditioning, heating and cooling of air, and with the provision of mobile and wireless communications equipment. Computers, once themselves the size of rooms, are now just threads, like thoughts, hidden in the architectural fabric.

Click. The windows above in the reading room have just started closing. I can hear the motors. But I can't see the windows. Actually, I can't tell whether it's dark outside or not, the temperature must have returned to its specified level. It is always bright enough, so it doesn't concern me what time it is.

References
1 Marshall Berman, *All That Is Solid Melts Into Air: the Experience of Modernity*, Verso (London), 1982, p 132.

Gout Clinic, Swindon

Michael Aling
Diploma Architecture (2008)
Tutors: *Nic Clear* and *Simon Kennedy*

The near future is presented in this project as a continuation and exaggeration of the postmodern 'cinematic society'. Set in the provincial UK town of Swindon, a social-economic experiment known as 'postindividualism' is under way. It is identifiable by: (a) A population of conjoined individuals; two or three people share a name and individuality. Individuals become 'roles' shared and acted out; (b) The death of the service economy; an entire demographic in middle-management positions mourn the death of retail; (c) A population rife with gout; the disease of consumption and excessive office hours; and (d) The construction of cinematic space. The first new-build in postindividualist Swindon, a gout medical facility, is constructed around the cinematic needs of a documentary film.

Greasy Spoon Café, Lincoln's Inn Fields

David Gouldstone
Diploma Architecture (2008)
Tutors: *Phil Ayres*, *Stephen Gage* and *James O'Leary*

This intense project is the culmination of a two-year investigation into the Picturesque and the influence of previous memories on the subsequent perception of place and space. Gouldstone's earlier projects were based on in-depth studies of Chiswick House and the Soane Museum. These studies included a personal notation of the underlying time base that drives this type of experience. 'Greasy Spoon Café' itself discloses an extraordinary ability to represent ideas in largely freehand drawings.

There is a strong emphasis on the physical presence of architecture, for the project incorporates the mundane reality of day-to-day activity and turns it into a world that can be perceived to be both plausible and surreal.

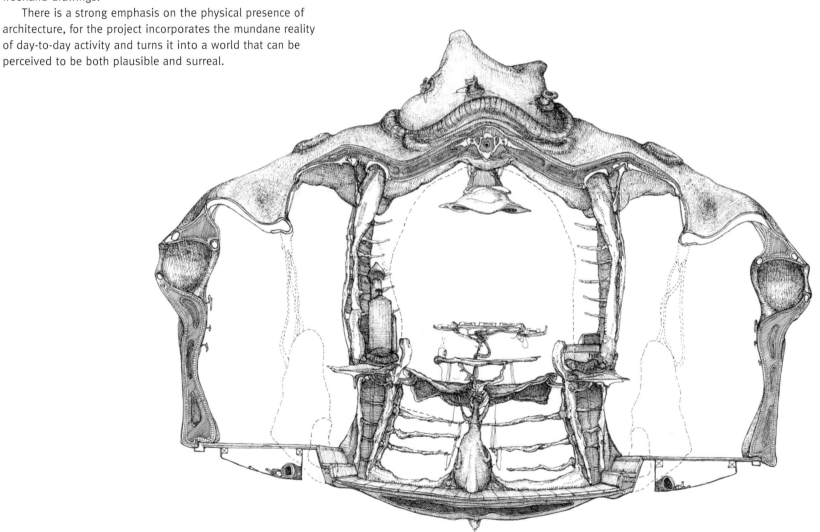

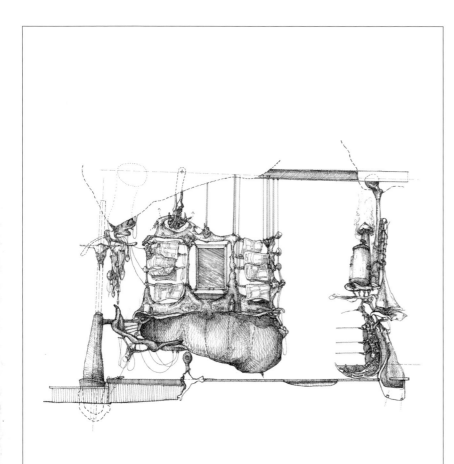

SECTION THROUGH AREA IN FRONT OF HIGH TEA
COUNTER SHOWING NEWSPAPER RACK AND SEATING AREA
FOR USE WHILE WAITING FOR ORDERS

HIGH TEA COUNTER
MAIN GRILL SHOWN BEHIND

Gulliver

Joerg Majer
Diploma Architecture (2006)
Tutors: *Simon Herron* and *Susanne Isa*

'Gulliver' is a constructed archive that takes a look at our architectural heritage, from the works of Robert Hooke through John Soane to Le Corbusier. Here, the archive is explored through multiple media, scales and techniques. Excavation is seen as a creative process where 'lost objects' are found.

These discoveries require imagination, continual interpretation, testing and reappraisal resulting in the emergence of architectural works that evolve over time. Half-truths, errors and built-in imperfections suggest the possibility for refinement and a demand to continually assess. As knowledge accrues, so does the scope, size and depth of the proposition. Technology appropriate to each era is deployed to understand what it is that has been uncovered. Finally, this technology is also used to create new physical propositions, where architecture literally becomes the body.

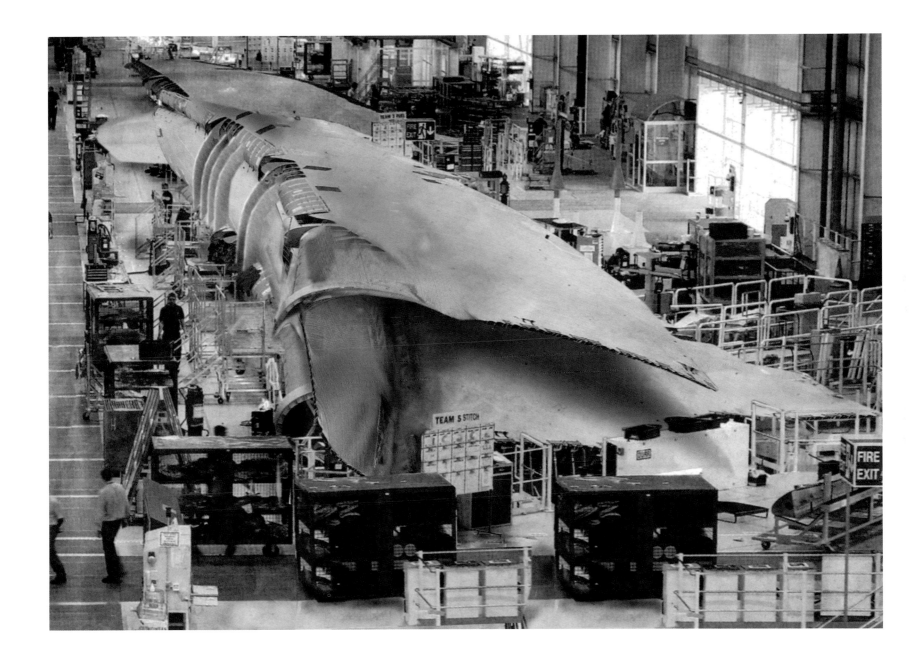

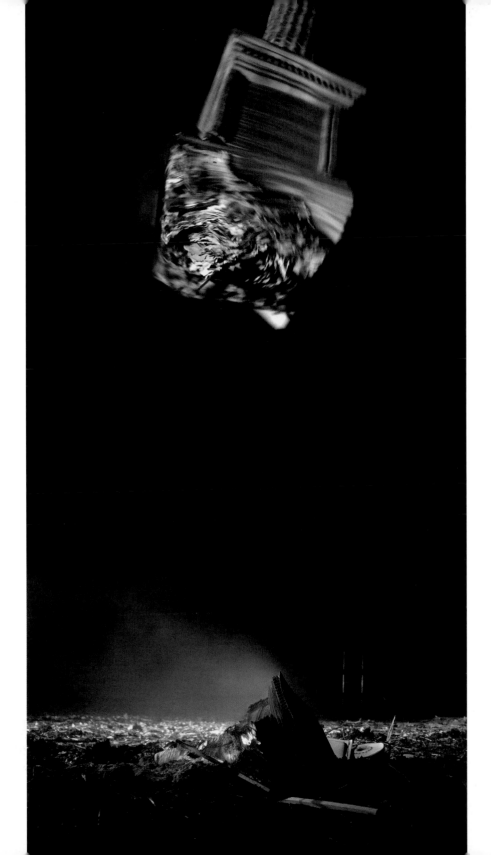

Hooke's Invisible Monument

Matt Wilkinson
Diploma Architecture (2008)
Tutors: *Simon Herron* and *Susanne Isa*

The project is initially conceived as a response to the notion that Robert Hooke's reputation has been overshadowed by that of Isaac Newton. It creates a monument to Hooke, dispersed across London. Each component of the monument uses one of Hooke's theories or discoveries to develop its architecture. The project also explores gravitational phenomena in order to distort space and time. In short, this is a fragmentary architecture of gravitational gradients and a London-wide mnemonic laboratory.

Horseriders' Hostel, Paracutin

Agnieszka Glowacka
Diploma Architecture (2002)
Tutors: *Niall McLaughlin* and *Yeoryia Manolopoulou*

The village of Paracutin has been engulfed by lava. Only the Baroque steeple of the church rises out of the dark mass of stone. This proposition is for a hostel at the nearby village of Angahuan, intended for visitors who would come to ride horses through this strange volcanic landscape. A properly developed tourist economy might then help to stem the damage that local inhabitants are doing to the forests by excessive logging. The project itself is an intense material investigation into the parts of a building. Lava blocks, water bags and braided coir tresses are worked into an arrangement that is both primitive and knowing. The simple myth of cowboys resting up under a cliff is elaborated into a series of strange constructions: in one, the horse and the rider sleep cheek by jowl, separated only by soft water-filled canteens; in another, both horse and rider wash in lava block caves with water welling up underneath. Rainwater is channelled through the coir roof to fill butts below. Seasonal downpours saturate the lava floor swelling bathing pools for horses.

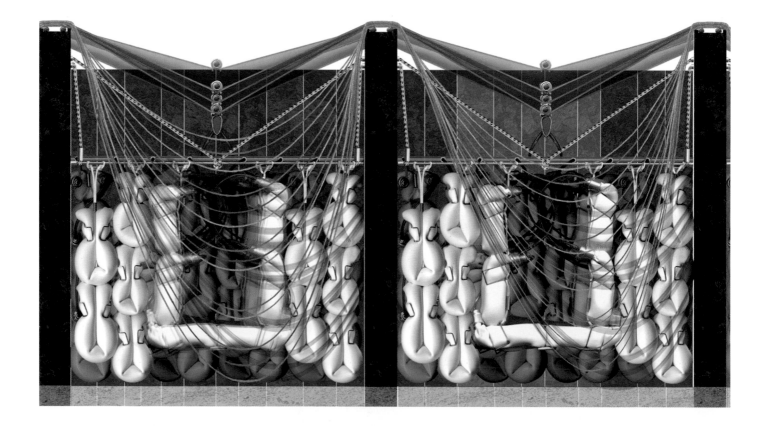

Hotel Room

Dora Sweijd
Diploma Architecture (2006)
Tutors: *Peter Culley* and *Christine Hawley*

This narrative project explores a hotel bedroom with its formulaic components and the action that takes place once a chambermaid enters the room. Hotel bedroom design is non-negotiable; so too are the acts of cleaning and bed-making, which are reduced to a systematic sequence of operations. Here, these actions are precisely choreographed. We are told of the maid's entry into a small box-like space, of the physiological action required to remove the sheets and then of the expansive movement undertaken as the new sheet billows out over the bed and slowly floats into place. The installation is a tall rectangular glass box set on a plinth. The room is darkened and we are asked to move around the box and look into the interior through two peepholes. As the audience assembles, the theatre is enacted. Multiple images of the sky, stars and a sleeping body are projected on to surfaces within the box.

Icelandic Parliament, Thingvellir

Ben Ridley
Diploma Architecture (2008)
Tutors: *Laura Allen* and *Mark Smout*

In this highly ambitious and complex project, a large and multi-faceted building manipulates the threshold between the synthetic and the natural, employing shifts in composition of landscape and architecture to provide a heightened sensory awareness of the Icelandic landscape.

Sited at Thingvellir, a World Heritage Site, and therefore designated as 'belonging to all people', the building has equally important political and social provisions: as a weekend retreat for migrant workers originating from warmer climes and who currently suffer under the unusual climatic conditions of the north of Iceland; and as a reconstruction of the parliamentary function of the historic site.

Physical and psychological comfort is provided by a series of mythically-inspired design devices, each of which encourages the development of the important psychological notions of belonging, comfort and attachment to landscape via the traditional Icelandic activity of inventing myth.

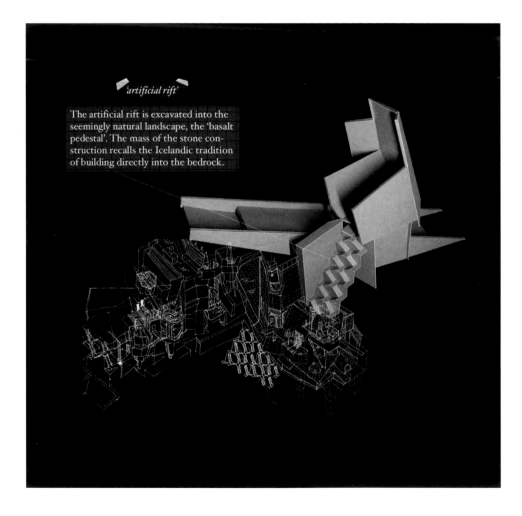

'artificial rift'

The artificial rift is excavated into the seemingly natural landscape, the 'basalt pedestal'. The mass of the stone construction recalls the Icelandic tradition of building directly into the bedrock.

● *golden gate*

The 'golden gate' accommodation follows the tradition of myth in ecclesiastical architecture. Such gateways traditionally represented passages of the sun to an underworld. Here the gates reflect sunlight, whilst enabling a view to the excavated landscape beneath

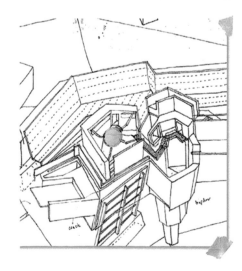

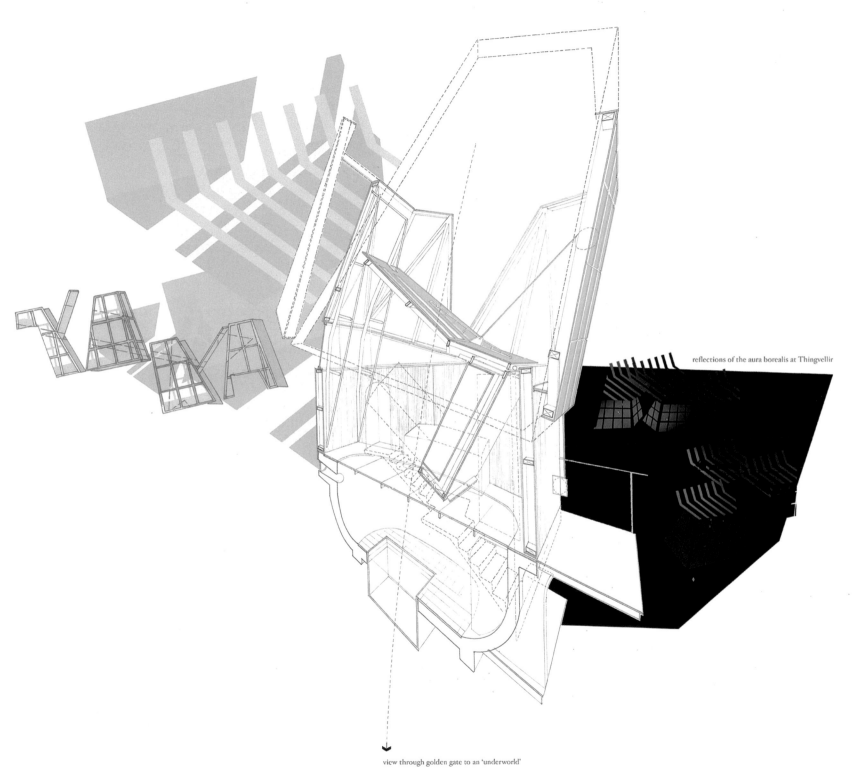

reflections of the aura borealis at Thingvellir

view through golden gate to an 'underworld'

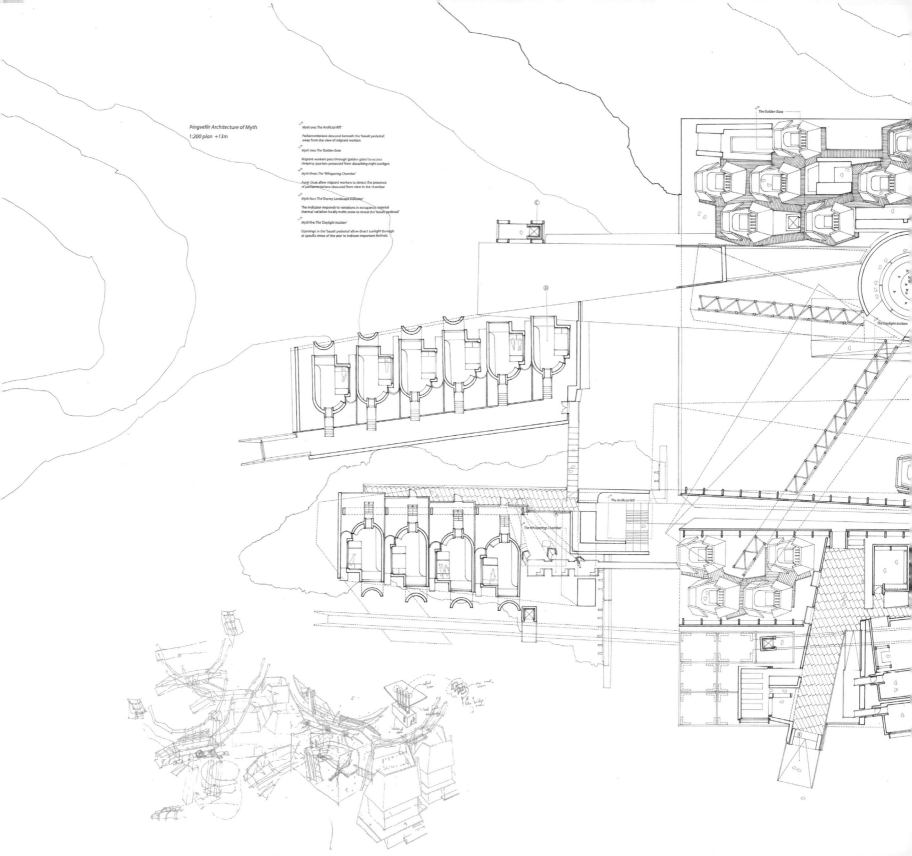

Þingvellir Architecture of Myth

1:200 plan +13m

Myth one: The 'Artificial Rift'

Parliamentarians descend beneath the 'basalt pedestal',
away from the view of migrant workers

Myth two: The 'Golden Gate'

Migrant workers pass through 'golden gates' to access
sleeping quarters protected from disturbing night sunlight

Myth three: The 'Whispering Chamber'

Aural clues allow migrant workers to detect the presence
of parliamentarians obscured from view in the chamber

Myth four: The 'Snowy Landscape Indicator'

The indicator responds to variations in occupancy; internal
thermal variation locally melts snow to reveal the 'basalt pedestal'

Myth five: The 'Daylight Incision'

Openings in the 'basalt pedestal' allow direct sunlight through
at specific times of the year to indicate important festivals

The Golden Gate

The Daylight Incision

The Artificial Rift

The Whispering Chamber

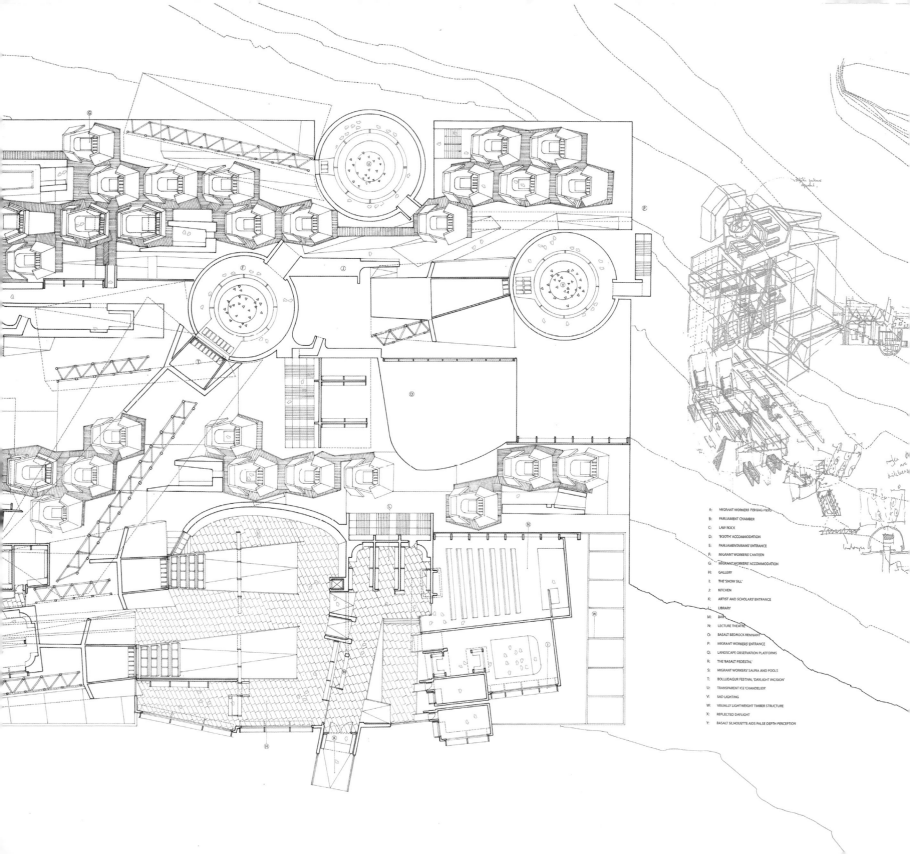

A: MIGRANT WORKERS' FISHING PIERS

B: PARLIAMENT CHAMBER

C: LAW ROCK

D: 'BOOTH' ACCOMMODATION

E: PARLIAMENTARIANS' ENTRANCE

F: MIGRANT WORKERS' CANTEEN

G: MIGRANT WORKERS' ACCOMMODATION

H: GALLERY

I: THE 'SNOW SILL'

J: KITCHEN

K: ARTIST AND SCHOLARS' ENTRANCE

L: LIBRARY

M: BAR

N: LECTURE THEATRE

O: BASALT BEDROCK REMNANT

P: MIGRANT WORKERS' ENTRANCE

Q: LANDSCAPE OBSERVATION PLATFORMS

R: THE 'BASALT PEDESTAL'

S: MIGRANT WORKERS' SAUNA AND POOLS

T: BOLLUDAGUR FESTIVAL 'DAYLIGHT INCISION'

U: TRANSPARENT ICE 'CHANDELIER'

V: SAD LIGHTING

W: VISUALLY LIGHTWEIGHT TIMBER STRUCTURE

X: REFLECTED DAYLIGHT

Y: BASALT SILHOUETTE AIDS FALSE DEPTH PERCEPTION

A: MIGRANT WORKERS' FISHING PIERS
B: PARLIAMENT CHAMBER
C: LAW ROCK
D: 'BOOTH' ACCOMMODATION
E: PARLIAMENTARIANS' ENTRANCE
F: MIGRANT WORKERS' CANTEEN
G: MIGRANT WORKERS' ACCOMMODATION
H: GALLERY
I: THE 'SNOW SILL'
J: KITCHEN
K: ARTIST AND SCHOLARS' ENTRANCE
L: LIBRARY
M: BAR
N: LECTURE THEATRE
O: BASALT BEDROCK REMNANT
P: MIGRANT WORKERS' ENTRANCE
Q: LANDSCAPE OBSERVATION PLATFORMS
R: THE 'BASALT PEDESTAL'
S: MIGRANT WORKERS' SAUNA AND POOLS
T: BOLLUDAGUR FESTIVAL 'DAYLIGHT INCISION'
U: TRANSPARENT ICE CHANDELIER'
V: SAD LIGHTING
W: VISUALLY LIGHTWEIGHT TIMBER STRUCTURE
X: REFLECTED DAYLIGHT
Y: BASALT SILHOUETTE AIDS FALSE DEPTH PERCEPTION

Þingvellir Architecture of Myth 1:200 section AA

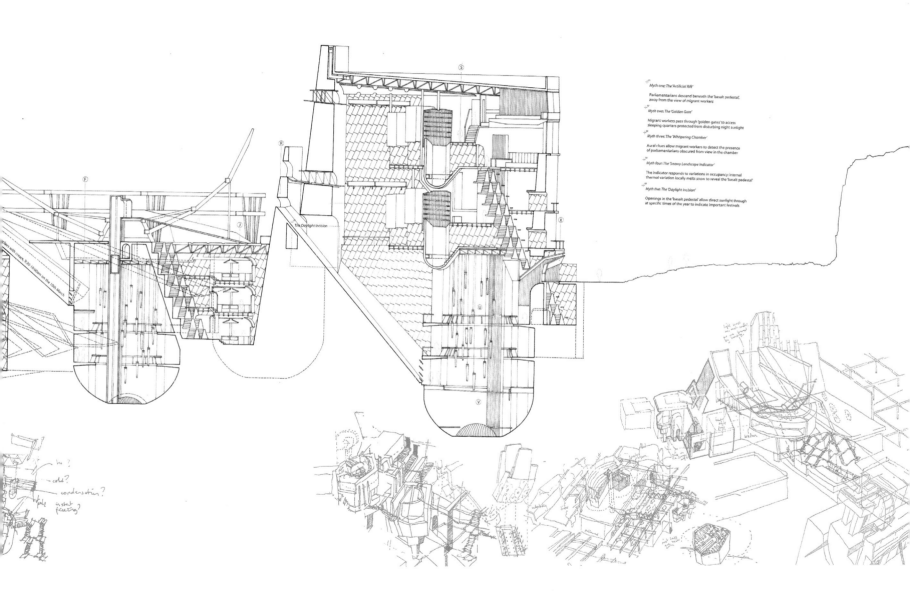

Myth one: The 'Artificial Rift'

Parliamentarians descend beneath the 'basalt pedestal', away from the view of migrant workers

Myth two: The 'Golden Gate'

Migrant workers pass through 'golden gates' to access sleeping quarters protected from disturbing night sunlight

Myth three: The 'Whispering Chamber'

Aural clues allow migrant workers to detect the presence of parliamentarians obscured from view in the chamber

Myth four: The 'Snowy Landscape Indicator'

The indicator responds to variations in occupancy: internal thermal variation locally melts snow to reveal the 'basalt pedestal'

Myth five: The 'Daylight Incision'

Openings in the 'basalt pedestal' allow direct sunlight through at specific times of the year to indicate important festivals

The Daylight Incision

Imagination

Jack Spencer Ashworth
BSc Architecture (2008)
Tutor: *Jan Birksted*

This BSc Architectural History and Theory essay explores how the intellectual and personal inclinations of imaginative writers affect their preconceptions of a place and, if so, how these inclinations manifest themselves in the text, specifically in the representation of architecture? The specific focus of the essay is the trip to Naples made by Walter Benjamin and Asja Lacis, who together conceived a 'law of porosity' in response to the city's architecture. Despite Lacis' obvious influence over Benjamin and her links with feminism, it appears that it was the city's modus vivendi that was the dominant factor.

We must go back to 1924. Benjamin has met Lacis and fallen in love with her. He is in turmoil emotionally but also intellectually. Lacis introduces him to, and persuades him with, new ideologies – in particular, communism. Is it possible that she also introduced him to marxist-feminism? So little seems to be known about Lacis' real intellectual ideals that it is uncertain. Lacis does appear to be a source of great interest to modern feminists, something of a heroine as a strong female figure who was successful in male-dominated communist Russia. If this is the case, then surely Lacis introduced Benjamin to the feminine concept of porosity, thus suggesting that the inclinations of the writers did affect their conceptions of Naples.

However, there are considerations that counteract this argument. The first is timing. There is no apparent description of a feminist concept of porous or fluid space so early on – it seems that it is a theory generated by 'second wave' feminists who appear in the early 1960s. In which case Benjamin and Lacis together came up with the original theory of porosity. One which was inspired by the city's architecture. This is supported by Claire Goldberg Moses's theory that feminists fabricate mythical heroes. She highlights a 'disjuncture between an American version of "French feminism" and an "actually existing feminism" in France'. Perhaps Lacis has been adopted as an early feminist by modern feminists, the same ones who have developed her (and Benjamin's) law of porosity?

The idea that it was an original concept is also supported by Benjamin's method of reflective judgement that, inspired by Alois Riegl, 'consists of a penetrating interpretation of the individual work which ... uncovers laws and problems of art as a whole'. In 'Naples', Benjamin's 'method of reflective judgement is that of the cameraman (the surgeon): as close-up shots of details are "assembled under a new law"'. As a method of ethnographic approach, this reflection might well produce such an organising technique as porosity.

Inhabitable Flesh of Architecture

Marcos Cruz
PhD Architectural Design (2007)
Supervisor: *Peter Cook*

The design-led PhD 'The Inhabitable Flesh of Architecture' is dedicated to a future vision of the body in architecture. It questions the contemporary relationship between human and architectural flesh. Conceptually, it delves into the arena of disgust on which the aesthetic flesh is standing, and it explores new types of 'neoplasmatic' conditions in which the future possibility of a neo-biological flesh is resting.

Through the analysis and design of a variety of projects, flesh is proposed as a concept that extends the meaning of skin, one of architecture's most fundamental metaphors. It seeks to challenge a common misunderstanding of skin as a flat and thin surface. In a time when a pervasive discourse about the impact of digital technologies risks turning the architectural 'skin' ever more disembodied, the aim of the thesis is to put forward a thick embodied flesh by exploring architectural interfaces that are truly inhabitable.

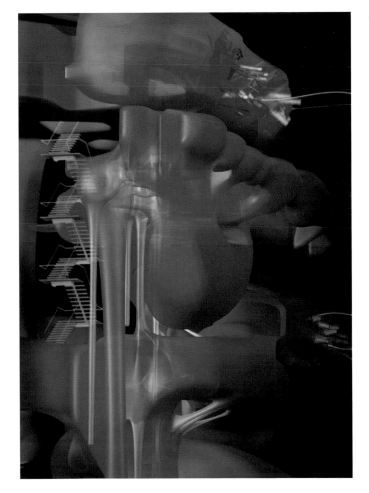

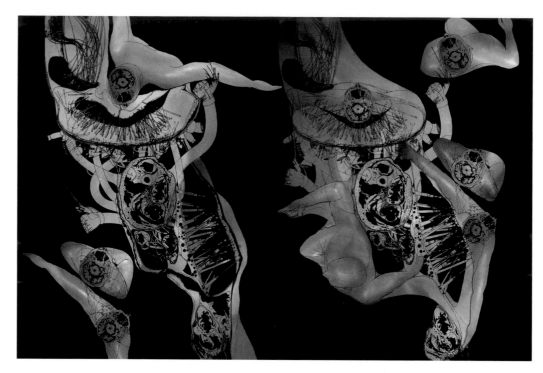

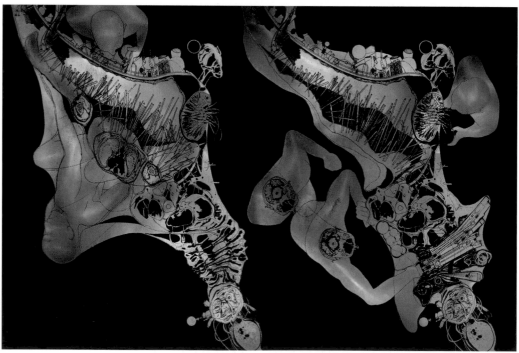

Inhabiting Infrastructures, Levittown

John Ashton
Diploma Architecture (2008)
Tutors: *Matthew Butcher, Elizabeth Dow* and *Jonathan Hill*

The project explores concepts of dwelling in a near-future no longer reliant on fossil fuel consumption. Sited in the satellite commuter town of Levittown outside New York, each house in the proposed community acts both as a home and, through daily occupation, as part of the town's infrastructure. These infrastructures manifest themselves as vast reservoir roofs collecting and storing rainwater, as large rotating mirrors capturing and reflecting every moment of daily sun, as basements drawing cold air from the earth, and as vast rubber stack chimneys storing up heat for redistribution during bitter winter nights. Drawing on local planning laws and the architectural vernacular of the American Midwest, the project presents a vulnerable but plausible near-future for dwelling in a world without oil.

Installation Projects

Year 1
BSc Architecture (2001–08)
Tutors: *Frosso Pimenides, Patrick Weber* and others

BSc Architecture Year 1 is structured around a series of projects, not all architectural in the conventional sense, which enable the students to be critical and inventive in the design of buildings. The installation project, undertaken in the very first three months of study, is the most challenging and fun of all.

Students investigate the design process as a collective experience of adjusting a given space. By quickly developing an idea from conception to built reality, working in groups, handling a limited budget, improvising with materials and suppliers, and working to an immovable deadline, the essence of both the reality and the magic of the building process is created. The means of this alchemy – a miraculous transformation of space – is the construction of a number of evocative, sometimes ephemeral, sometimes permanent structures responding to adjusting light and movement.

The installation project has evolved over several years, beginning with a surrealist banquet where experiences are 'served up', developing into a sequence of carefully choreographed spatial narratives, to its present form of free-standing interventions which are in place for a full evening – or longer. The conventions of the feast and the sensual architecture of the temporary are always a strong reference. These installations help to develop a design process from an ideal proposition, from the constraints of fabrication and materiality, and from all sorts of eccentric personal observations. They are an act of learning by doing, in which students are engaged with the physical and tactile nature of architecture.

Instrumental Architectures

Kyle Buchanan
Diploma Architecture (2008)
Tutors: *Laura Allen* and *Mark Smout*

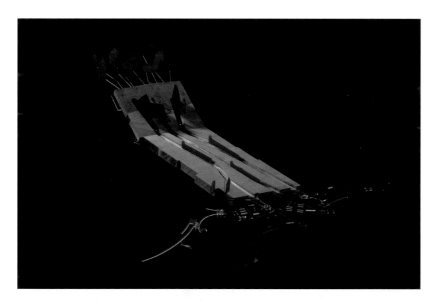

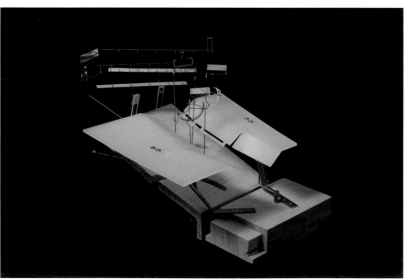

This project takes two conceptual routes by which to scrutinise site and social context in the liminal regions of the estuaries of the east of England. First, the project examines the pressing contemporary problem of rising sea levels with reference to historic examples, existing constructions and current propositions. Second, the project determines a working method that draws from 17th-century navigational tools of scientific experimentation and discovery. As a result, idealised environments and beautiful exquisite instruments combine technical inventiveness and landscape reconfiguration with architectural proposals — machines, site and their use become entwined.

The 'Super-Sextant' is sited at Canvey Island in the Thames Estuary. By means of optical devices, weighted and counterbalanced platforms, the scheme penetrates the wall that, since its construction in the 1950s, has dislocated the land from the sea and the islanders from the distant horizon.

The 'Jam Port and Instrumental Architecture' proposal is sited, 50 years hence, at Tollesbury in the vulnerable Essex Blackwater Estuary, where contentious land management schemes – such as techniques of managed realignment – are being tested. These offer a 'sustainable' alternative to sea defence by sharing land with the sea. The project proposes a relocation of food manufacture and distribution that moves from international and intensive systems to more local configurations. The 'instrument' uses the tides and passive energy to entwine the fabric of the port with the wet edge of the land.

The work deploys machinic viewing devices with lenses that focus, enlarge and distort, and prisms that bend views and triangulate trajectories. These delicate and ingenious assemblages, constructed with an explicit degree of patience and inimitable tooling, underline the precision, appropriateness and responsivity of the architecture.

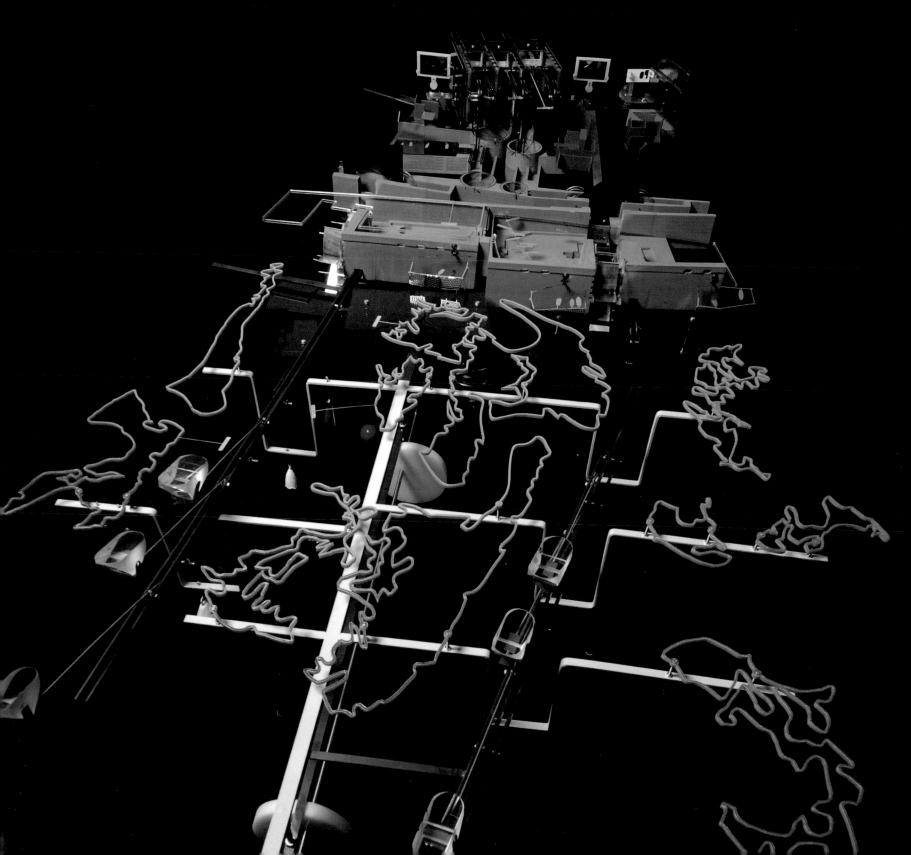

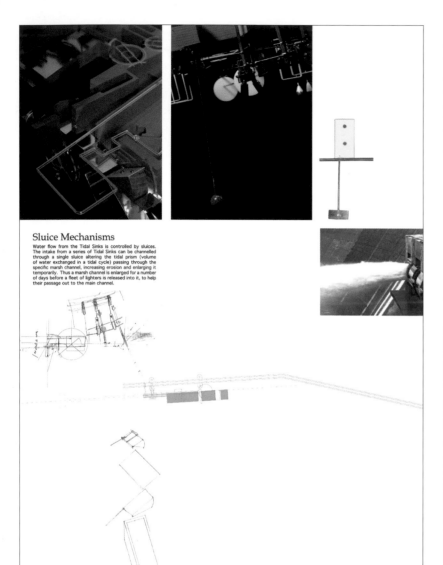

Sluice Mechanisms

Water flow from the Tidal Sinks is controlled by sluices. The intake from a series of Tidal Sinks can be channelled through a single sluice altering the tidal prism (volume of water exchanged in a tidal cycle) passing through the specific marsh channel, increasing erosion and enlarging it temporarily. Thus a marsh channel is enlarged for a number of days before a fleet of lighters is released into it, to help their passage out to the main channel.

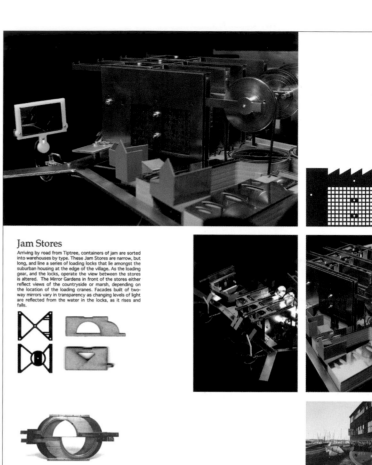

Jam Stores

Arriving by road from Tiptree, containers of jam are sorted into warehouses by type. These Jam Stores are narrow, but long, and line a series of loading locks that lie amongst the suburban housing at the edge of the village. As the loading gear, and the locks, operate the view between the stores is altered. The Mirror Gardens in front of the stores either reflect views of the countryside or marsh, depending on the location of the loading cranes. Facades built of two-way mirrors vary in transparency as changing levels of light are reflected from the water in the locks, as it rises and falls.

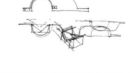

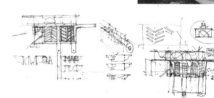

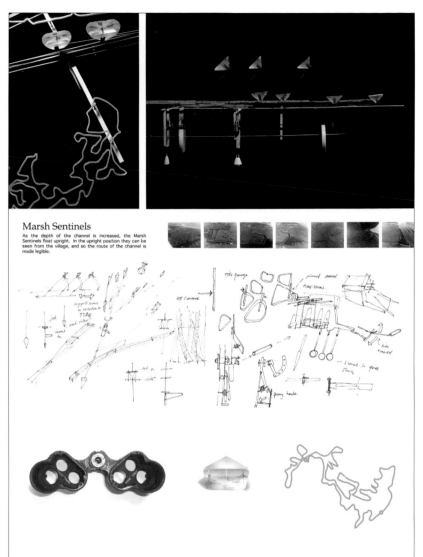

Marsh Sentinels

As the depth of the channel is increased, the Marsh Sentinels float upright. In the upright position they can be seen from the village, and so the route of the channel is made legible.

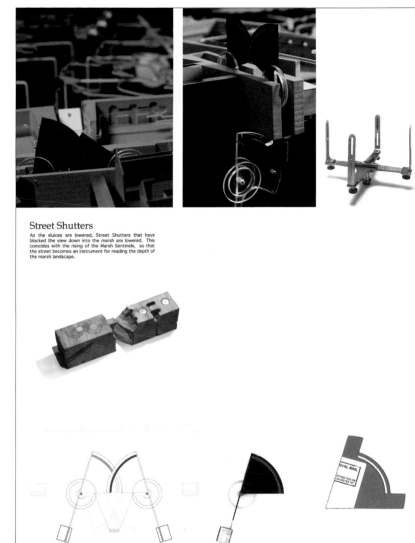

Street Shutters

As the sluices are lowered, Street Shutters that have blocked the view down into the marsh are lowered. This coincides with the rising of the Marsh Sentinels, so that the street becomes an instrument for reading the depth of the marsh landscape.

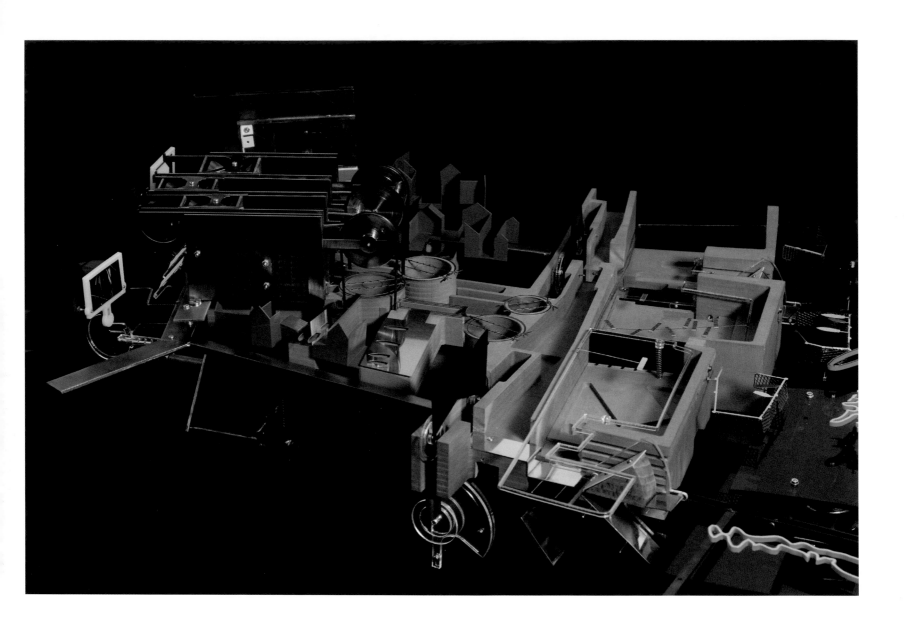

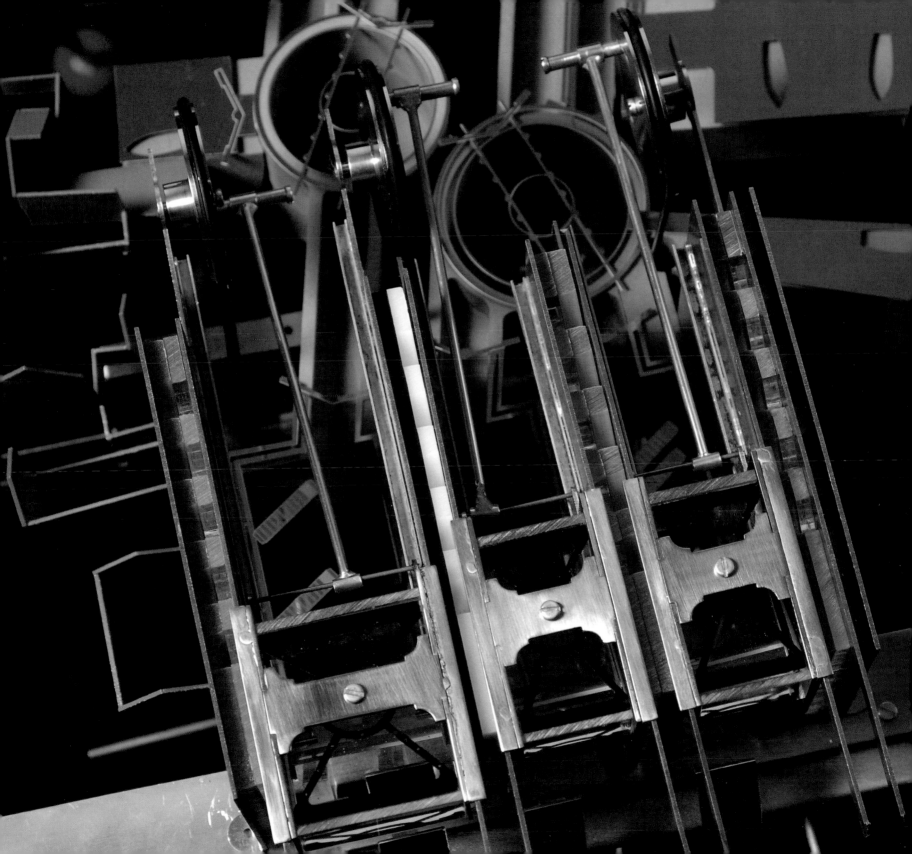

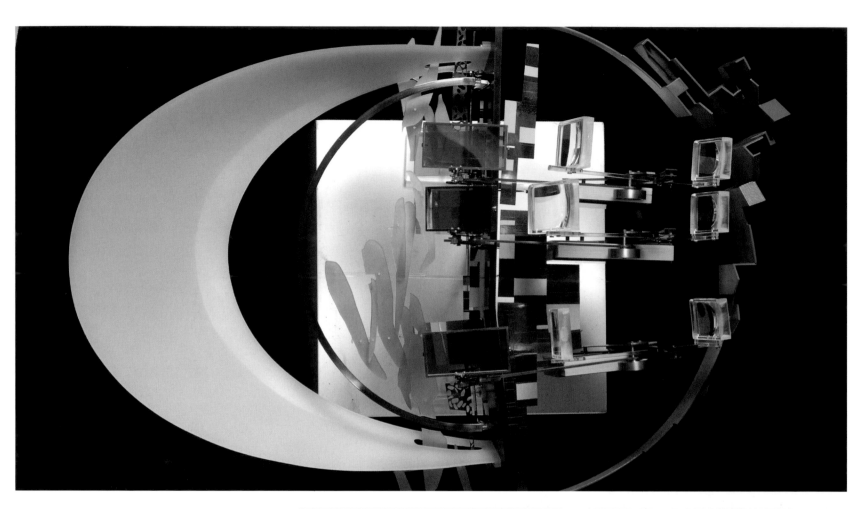

Intensive Care Installation

Ian David
Diploma Architecture (2004)
Tutors: *Bob Sheil*, *Zoe Smith* and *Graeme Williamson*

The project is one of a series of installations at the former Queen Elizabeth Children's Hospital, now a dilapidated and abandoned assembly of unoccupied rooms in the Hackney area of London. A dense cluster of unique fragile plaster castings is created, where each piece is either suspended or supported from precarious stainless-steel rods. The work recognises the present sense of delicate decay as the hospital slides into a weak and hazardous condition. The castings randomly smash to the floor as slight changes in temperature or air circulation disturb their environment.

Interaction

Marcos Cruz and **Stephen Gage**

Architecture is always a matter of interaction between fabric, spaces and people. Here we suggest two discrete yet interrelated ways by which this interaction might occur: 'Performance and Magic' and 'Inhabitable Interfaces'.

Performance and Magic

The American anthropologist, author and actor William Beeman describes how performance is both mimetic (in that it imitates action) and affective (in that it transforms action). An anthropological view of performance is that it encompasses all institutions of public behaviour, including those which control and direct ritual and social interactions. The built environment thus contains both the settings and the props for the performance of the everyday. Taken together, this forms the physical interfaces discussed below. Beeman describes how performance is always 'emergent', but 'in the context of the ground rules for the conduct of performance that make up the structured system of conventional performance for the community'. This is close to concepts of emergence that are derived from the agent-based representation of social interaction.

Gregory Bateson (1904–80) – the British anthropologist, social scientist, linguist, semiotician and cyberneticist – described the notion of 'framing' in his essay 'A Theory of Play and Fantasy' (1955).[1] Bateson explains that play is a quintessential example of 'framed behaviour', whose individuals regulate their behaviour according to a set of rules that operate only as long as the play frame is in force. The concept of framing has recently been used as a tool in the construction of multi-agent software systems. The concept can also apply very directly to the built environment, as long as it is recognised that the frame contains both a physical construct (physical interface) and a cluster of congruent mental constructs. The latter are expressed in predictable behaviours. It could be argued that social behaviours are the product of the interaction of autonomous agents, as a 'bottom up' approach. The production of a building, however, is generally thought to be a 'top down'

process, even if the reality is in fact much more complex than simply involving a large number of stakeholders each performing a very specific role. The ethical problem of a 'top down' approach was neatly sidestepped by the software designer and performer Paul Pangaro in his paper 'Pask as Dramaturg' (1993).[2] In this paper, Pangaro describes the top down approach as 'organisational modelling', identifying the essentially autopoeisic quality that underlies the creation of a performance that did not previously exist. What are the basic characteristics of a theatrical top down system? A minimum meta-description of a top down social system includes 'creators of' and 'observers in' the system. The 'creators of' the system both design the system and find the initial resources to make it happen. The 'observers in' the system are either 'active' or 'passive' – and the distinction between active and passive is critical.

An explicit consideration of audience and illusion leads us to consider the relationship between the practice of stage magic and the creation of both physical and 'virtual' architecture – and it is significant that Bruce Tognazzini, a specialist in human-computer interaction design, finds an eerie correspondence between the two: 'Perhaps no field other than magic is tied so closely to the field of graphical interface design: the people working at Xerox PARC in the 1960s and early 1970s were aware of the principles of theatrical magic when creating the first graphical interfaces, to the extent that David Smith named the interface itself the "user illusion". [...] We are designing interfaces for an interface system based on magic, yet there is almost nothing written about it in our literature. [...] Magicians have been struggling with the principles, techniques, and ethics of illusion for at least 5000 years. There's a lot we can learn from them.'[3] Magicians and digital interface designers have no problem with the idea that a 'real world' exists 'out there', from which metaphors can be drawn that will convince their audiences. Designers and architects, however, might be uncomfortable with this opportunistic notion. Their discomfort would be natural – because they construct the 'real world' from which many of the metaphors are drawn, and can, in principle, change it if they wish. This is where the parallels between stage magic and architecture are closer than those between stage magic and interface design as understood by Tognazzini.

Inhabitable Interfaces

Modern architecture has been concerned mainly with the use and design of 'empty' space, ideally unrestricted by mass and matter. As a result, walls (and by and large the physical substance of architecture) have been socially, politically and functionally relegated to the status of being mere space organisers and dividers. But there is more to be said about what is actually hidden behind our contemporary physical surrounding, in particular the interactive potential of inhabitable interfaces. Contrary to the widespread idea that interfaces are purely digital phenomena, these interfaces should be understood instead as physical constructs with, and in which, people interact. Hence, 'inhabitable interfaces' are understood as an extended meaning of walls. Involving both a mental and physical activity, 'inhabitable' is a condition that is ever transient, and implies the potential act of becoming inhabited. It suggests an embodied experience, which is the interplay between the body's presence, its perceptual practice, and the engagement with the environment around it. Due to their centrally programmatic role, but their often-peripheral location in buildings, the characters of such spaces can be considered as intrinsically 'sociofugal' – a term originally used by the American anthropologist Edward T Hall, for whom this suggests a drive away from social interaction. But when bearing in mind the performative and magic potential of inhabitable interfaces, one could also argue that these places are rather 'sociopetal' promoting individual engagement and social interaction in the liminal substance of architecture.

There is a rich history of buildings in which interfacial inhabitation has been applied, not just through the thickening of walls and facades as containers (such as built-in storage and in-wall seating), but also the masking of intimate life understood as both a voyeuristic and haptic experience. Moreover, there is also the bodily engagement with increasingly artificial and environmentally controlled spaces, the dressing of buildings reduced to capsules or suits, the inhabitation of media facades, or the spiritual immersion into the spatial and ornamental depth of nooks, niches and alcoves in sacred spaces.

All in all, inhabitable interfaces are part of a history that has always promoted the reciprocating engagement of body and architecture, ie the body understood as an extension of buildings, and vice versa. This 'wallist' approach prompts a conceptual shift from a space-centric to a wall-centric (and ultimately body-centric) understanding of architecture. Inhabitable interfaces, as defined here, entail conditions that generate an intensive experience, as well as haptic awareness, of our surrounding space. They create an expanded boundary in which the notion of being inhabitable is a catalyst of both individual activity and social performance, at the same time creating a receptacle of a projected life that is vital to our sense of intimacy in a more pleasurable dimension of architecture.

References
1   Gregory Bateson, 'A Theory of Play and Fantasy', *Psychiatric Research Reports*, n 2 (1955), pp 39–51.
2   Paul Pangaro, 'Pask as Dramaturg', *Systems Research*, v 10, n 3 (1993), pp 135–42.
3   Bruce Tognazzini, 'Principles, Techniques, and Ethics of Stage Magic and Their Application to Human Interface Design', *Proceedings of INTERCHI* (Amsterdam: 24–9 April 1993), pp 355–62.

Interactive Devices

Philip Waind
Diploma Architecture (2001)
Tutors: *Stephen Gage* and *Will Mclean*

Do we attribute emotion and intention to things? Do they appear to be surrounded by 'object space' in the same way that we are surrounded by 'personal space'? This project suggests that this is especially the case with interactive objects. The installation consists of active veneer fans, which react to each other as a social group. Supplementary interactive objects, in the form of human participants, can become incorporated into the group.

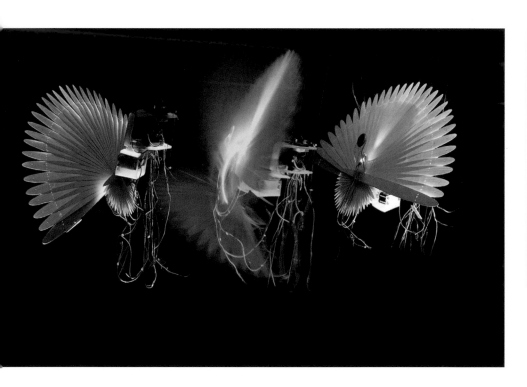

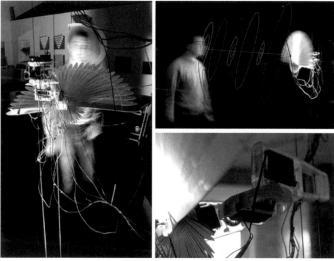

Intimate Encounter

Lilian Chee
PhD Architectural History and Theory (2006)
Supervisor: *Jane Rendell*

The question of experience, including the researcher's reflexive entanglement with her subject matter, is frequently excluded from architectural epistemology, especially in architectural history. This PhD – 'An Architecture of Intimate Encounter: Plotting the Raffles Hotel Through Flora and Fauna, 1887–1925 and 1987–2005' – therefore reconfigures the 'architectural subject' as a relational double-entity inscribed through a network of spaces and times holding together the experiencing subject (researcher, writer, critic, historian, theorist or occupant) and her architectural object of study.

The intimate encounter also describes a methodology, which expands the repertoire of architectural evidence. It reclaims inventive forms of evidence – such as anecdotes, fictions, rumour, gossip and trivia – which are central to popular perceptions of a space like Singapore's colonial Raffles Hotel but which are ultimately repressed in its architectural histories.

Specifically, the thesis explores how two 'trivial' historical architectural facts – the hotel's relationship with writer W Somerset Maugham who fabricated stories of the 'exotic east' in the hotel's Palm Court, and a trail of true but bizarre animal tales – could potentially transform, undermine or corroborate its idealised architectural representations. Within the context of a monument's history, this feminist-influenced approach also challenges how an 'architectural subject' is defined. Here, the hotel is not an a priori subject, since the architectural subject unfolds only as a consequence of an encounter with Maugham and the animals.

The writing is informed by two parallel voices. An academic argument is punctuated at various points by creative texts and objects, a fugitive archive drawn from the hotel's past, thus underscoring how archival materials are public yet private, factual yet fictive. Despite their proximity, there is no attempt to make one voice reciprocally annotate or illustrate the other. Instead, each voice forwards different modalities and questions, thus reflecting how architectural meaning-making delicately negotiates between experience and deliberation.

Island Works

Harriet Lee
Diploma Architecture (2007)
Tutors: *Phil Ayres, Stephen Gage* and *James O'Leary*

Initial delight and wonder can pall. A question therefore arises as to how trivial or non-trivial machines can be constructed so that the output is continually surprising and new. Simple ways of achieving this might be derived from time-based media, especially dynamic sculpture and performance art. However, both of these examples rely on essentially predictable processes. By placing the constructed project in the context of a wider changing environment and treating the output of the system as deriving from both, less predictable outputs can be achieved. This project shows, in an exquisite melding of the natural and the artificial, how a construct can evoke a sense of mystery and grace.

James Bond Tableau

Doug Hodgson, Imran Jahn, Emma James, Arati Khanna and **Poppy Kirkwood**
Diploma Architecture (2006)
Tutors: *Peter Culley* and *Christine Hawley*

A full-scale tableau depicts a fictional encounter between James Bond and the evil temptress, where anticipation, action, time and outcome are captured through a combination of physical symbolism and constructed metaphors. The mood is set by a table laid for two. Players are represented by complex mechanisms, wine is consumed, oysters are decoratively presented on translucent plates, poison is deployed. But the plot is foiled and Bond escapes with his life. The scene is enacted in a rooftop restaurant with a combination of Victorian-esque mechanisms, wax plates, a miniaturised chandelier and a mood-changing canopy that casts differing colours over the setting. The 'James Bond Tableau' project-event is accompanied by an immediately recognisable movie score, creating an evocative filmic sequence.

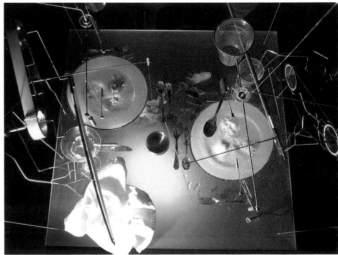

Land of Scattered Seeds

John Puttick
Diploma Architecture (2001)
Tutors: *Colin Fournier* and *Peter Szczepaniak*

This project for the city of Graz was developed in response to a brief for an urban microcosm, an architectural intervention that would be extremely dense and contain an intense cross-section of urban activities. The 'Land of Scattered Seeds', suggesting an outrageous parasitic vegetal invasion of a quiet provincial town, instigated by colourful characters who wish to supplement their income by a semi-illicit parallel economy, is a brilliantly orchestrated series of events. It clearly departs, conceptually and stylistically, from accepted norms and yet is executed with great professionalism and precision. The work was originally presented in the form of a model and as a voluminous book.

Two brothers, Franz and Jorg, have lived on Sackstrasse at the foot of the Schlossberg all their lives. Depressed by the emptiness of their working routine and desperate to add to their income, the pair dream of becoming farmers. Using the only space they have available – outside their apartment buildings – the brothers go into production. Franz establishes a vineyard, while Jorg grows pumpkins to refine into Kurbisol. The two maniacally compete.

Across the street live Olga and Florian, who retired from the civil service five years ago. Horrified by the vegetal chaos erupting in the area, the couple cultivate formal gardens on the facade of their building as an act of floral defence. Lola, owner of the local hairdressing salon, proves more enterprising – taking the petals shed from Franz's vines to produce an enriching shampoo. As time passes the area flourishes – the farmers exploit the terrain to provide irrigation, and Franz has to use all his resources to persuade other local characters (Stefan, Helga, Hermann, Hugo and Wolf) of the merits of his scheme. All the while, wild plants and birds continue to invade and so the struggles of Franz, Jorg, Olga, Florian and Lola continue ...

Hermann the bird man.

For some time wild birds have stolen the grapes that Franz has cultivated. Gathering his courage, the timid bird lover suggests one solution - an aviary.

Stefan & Helga.

Stefan & Helga were delighted by the Pergola they had insisted that Franz construct. The space enclosed will be perfect for our Cocktail and Conasta parties, they agreed. Fifi loved her new space too.

Landscape

Laura Allen and **Yeoryia Manolopoulou**

It is perhaps surprising that a great deal of architectural education still tends to view landscape and architecture as two separate areas of study – and that, very often, landscape is treated as a separate specialisation of design and theory. However, if we consider landscape in relation to the notion of place and to the definition of boundaries, we will see its direct relation – whether visual, geographical, cultural or political – to architecture and to the built environment. Moreover, our understanding of landscape should not be separated from our conception of spatial and temporal phenomena at large. In short, landscape plays a fundamental role in how we construct architectural thinking.

For a long time, the UCL Bartlett School of Architecture has recognised the significance of landscape as being inseparable from architectural design. It has opposed the distinction between landscape and architecture as being false, and has explored instead new architectures which fuse the two categories: bleak lands become intense architectural propositions, interiors become exteriors, complex cities become gardens, and vice versa. Environment and building, the 'natural' and the 'man-made', are combined in critical and inventive dialogue in projects that ask what architecture is or can be.

The long-held and romantic perception of landscape as a scene of uncorrupted nature often informs our relationship with the built environment. However, landscapes are never still. Landscapes are dynamic environments constructed again and again throughout history in response to continuously fluxing forces, different cycles and varying speeds. They change subtly through everyday occupation, weathering and climate, and dramatically because of political and cultural reasons. They are partly 'becoming' and partly 'vanishing'. Landscape's apparent ameliorative power to illuminate and revive even the most dismal of territories adds to the sense that our natural surroundings are anything but neutral and that our response to them is – or should be – far from dispassionate. Marry this understanding of landscape with the accumulating global momentum of nature's forces and we can see why, at the Bartlett, the experience of landscape and the environment pervades many student projects, from the hands-on site-specific installations and mappings of BSc Architecture Year 1 to innovative theoretical and design-based research at PhD level.

One of the earliest uses of the term landscape is in 16th-century painting, where people were introduced to idealised landscapes through paintings rather than through their own lived experiences of places. Nearly five centuries later, the Bartlett explores landscape's relation to scenery in a totally different spirit. Texts, drawings, models and time-based pieces are often consciously constructed as analogies to landscapes, in order to move beyond representation to original and polemical architectural propositions. Intense expeditions to various destinations – from under-defined London sites to far-away places in China or Brazil – enrich and test the projects against a diversity of topographies and cultures.

Ben Ridley's project 'Icelandic Parliament', for example, manipulates the synthetic and the natural to create equally important political and social provisions for a large, multi-faceted building, designated as 'belonging to all people' at a World Heritage Site in Iceland. Essentially, this is an architectural reconstruction of parliament and landscape via the theme of Icelandic myth. James Daykin's 'Salt Youth Hostel' project on the extreme climate of the Utah desert, on the other hand, is conceived as a monolithic earthwork of mud and salt, a material geology that preserves the building, yet weathers the landscape, making nature from artifice which in turn will return to nature.

In this book, there is an enormous variety of landscape typologies on which to gaze. We scrutinise the melancholic distance — the vast expanse and the empty horizon where scale and temporality are key – as well as industrial topographies where the human desire to dominate and transform nature is imperative. Either way, the landscape offers raw materials and undisciplined environments with which architecture must contend. One could say that landscape is reclaimed by architecture, that architecture provides a substitute materiality, and adds a strange flavour to site where one state is transformed into another. On the other hand, architecture can provide a kind of benign equivalence, a complement to fluid landscape by which the complexity of our relationship with a place can be measured.

Architecture can act as a generative agent for our perception of the environment. As authors and architects we influence the porosity of architecture to the phenomena of nature, altering where light falls, when shadows play, if dust rises, and how materials colour. Modifying our environmental sensitivity exposes architecture's ability to respond to, and reflect, the fundamental irrepressibility of nature, producing, in architectural space, a kaleidoscopic array of events by which architecture is propelled into life. We can create illusionistic reverberations in the otherwise inert and resistant material of architecture. Things might not be quite what they seem. An unnerving echo, the ricochet of sound on space, can be constructed to allude to unseen melodious expanses of uninhabited space; a draught circulated over cool surfaces condenses to form rivulets from thin air; a minuscule change may evoke memory and significant psychological attachment to place. The individuality of experience and of our imagination can allow space to seem substantially altered by percipient environmental design.

Implicit in here are much deeper concerns – for each body moves in a 'point-horizon' structure which, according to the French phenomenological philosopher Maurice Merleau-Ponty (1908–61), is the foundation of space. The horizon defines the limits of human vision and, metaphorically, the limits of knowledge. But a boundary is also that from which something begins its presence. Beyond the horizon, a new ground starts. A deeper consideration of the term landscape may hence suggest the origins and limits of architectural thought.

We have become comfortable with the notion that architecture presents an impenetrable and protective barrier to the external world, a reassuring ability to resist the rigours of the environment. But, bridging between the substance of architecture and our experience of space is the indeterminate and intangible liquid of 'immaterial' matter, through which architecture can become a modified body, a living environment. The English architect Cedric Price (1934–2003) showed how new architectural ideas need not be disconnected from political and cultural change. In a similar spirit, the projects shown here are uncompromised, in that they explore a synthesis of imagination and critique that fundamentally aims at the empowerment of places.

London After the Rain

Ben Olszyna-Marzys
Diploma Architecture (2007)
Tutors: *Nic Clear* and *Simon Kennedy*

'London After The Rain', as the name suggests, is a reference to Max Ernst's iconic painting *Europe After The Rain*. This architecture-as-film creates a bizarre post-industrial landscape, where the city has become overgrown and inhabited by a strange vision of humanity, accompanied by a variety of unlikely beasts.

Using collage techniques of juxtaposition, blended into a single homogeneous spatial construct, 'London After the Rain' taps into contemporary concerns with economic collapse and environmental degradation. So while the piece is playful in its construction, its overall theme is one of tremendous brooding anxiety.

Living Tower, New York

Rory Harmer
Diploma Architecture (2008)
Tutors: *David Ardill* and *Colin Fournier*

A new ecology is emerging in New York City, an 'architecture of becomings', an ecology that cultivates empiricism through the experience of being, nurturing new possibilities and discoveries. Growing out of the concrete and steel urban jungle, a mycelium of living structures evolves into the 'verdurous meta-market', a market that re-establishes 28th Street at the heart of New York's historic flower district. Scent, colour, vibrancy and diversity create a coalescence of sensorial perception, a stimulation of the senses bringing about the affects of spatiality. Through dynamic interaction and seasonal change, the meta-market gradually mutates the urban fabric of Manhattan into vertical pastures.

Luxor by Horse

Dimitrios Argyros
Diploma Architecture (2007)
Tutors: *Bernd Felsinger* and *cj Lim*

An eco-friendly and sustainable transport system of horse-and-carriage is proposed for Luxor's city centre to help alleviate the city's fast growing problems of urban congestion, pollution and animal welfare. The programme provides jobs for the many unemployed locals – as carriage drivers and as farmers to provide vast amounts of animal feed.

Due to the city's density, the transport union takes the form of a layered urban oasis – the natural and artificial undulating landscape has provision for resting facilities for the drivers, tower stables for 1,000 horses, and storage areas for food and recycling of animal waste. The horse stable tower recreates a natural equine environment while adopting the role of a national beacon of environmental sustainability and recycling.

The building is covered with local hand-made adobe bricks, made from horse manure – hence employing both new imported technologies and re-workings of traditional brick-making techniques. This manure-adobe brick both forms an insulating dry facade and also creates a sustainable and responsive greening facade, requiring no added water, soil, fertiliser or stabilising structure, and from which horses can feed during their daily wash and rest.

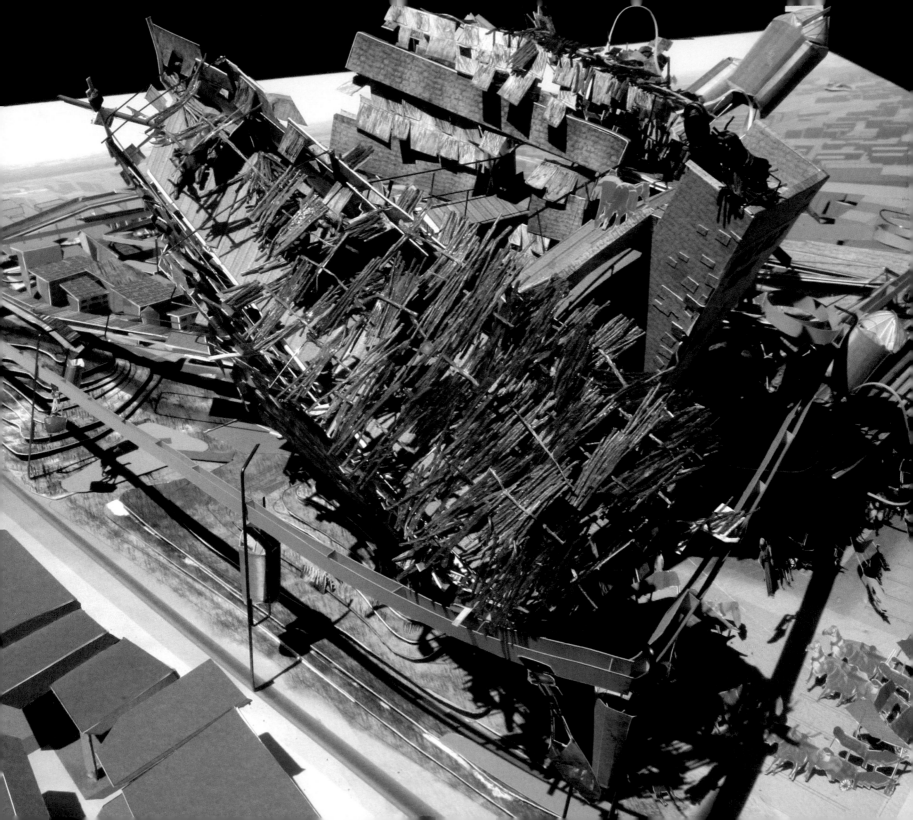

Made in China

Jimmy Hung
Diploma Architecture (2006)
Tutors: *Bernd Felsinger* and *cj Lim*

'Made in China' is a political satire focused on China's growing political power and its seemingly unstoppable economic strength. Cheap Chinese exports have caused the Western garment industry to collapse and have threatened the world's wider economy. This building is conceived as a powerful political reminder of the economic situation, the ship-like structure being a vast garment factory, where visitors and fashion buyers can shop for bespoke or mass-produced tailored suits and shirts at rock-bottom prices. Sited at the pier of Victoria Harbour on Hong Kong Island, 'Made in China' extends the already-vast shopping empire of Hong Kong's Central District, and hence acts as a bridge between China and the former British-governed colony of Hong Kong.

Magicians' Theatre, Rome

Sara Shafiei
Diploma Architecture (2007)
Tutors: *Marjan Colletti* and *Marcos Cruz*

The narrative background of this project begins by exploring Harry Houdini's 'Vanishing Elephant' trick, and specifically how this trick might be manifested within Albrecht Dürer's 'cone of vision'. The design readdresses the sensuality, three-dimensional depth and ornamental richness of the Italian Baroque. Notions of magical illusion and geometric anamorphosis generate surgically-constructed laser-cut models which describe both the functional solution of the circulation, and the spatial complexity of projections, performances and illusions.

The building is based on a site in the National Botanical Gardens in Rome. Text- and cone-anamorphosis, along with dispersed perspectival illusion, are used to create landscapes and ornamental tectonics that are revealed only to the dynamic user. Architecture here is not about frills, gadgetry or technicalities. It is constructed, choreographed and contemporary, structural and stylistic, experimental and experiential. It is secret, sacred and sublime.

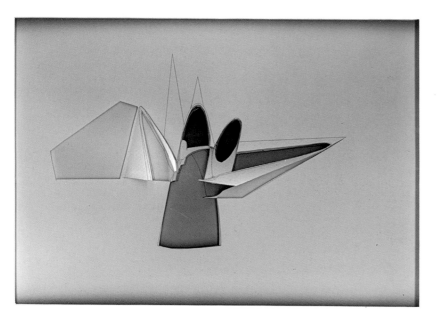

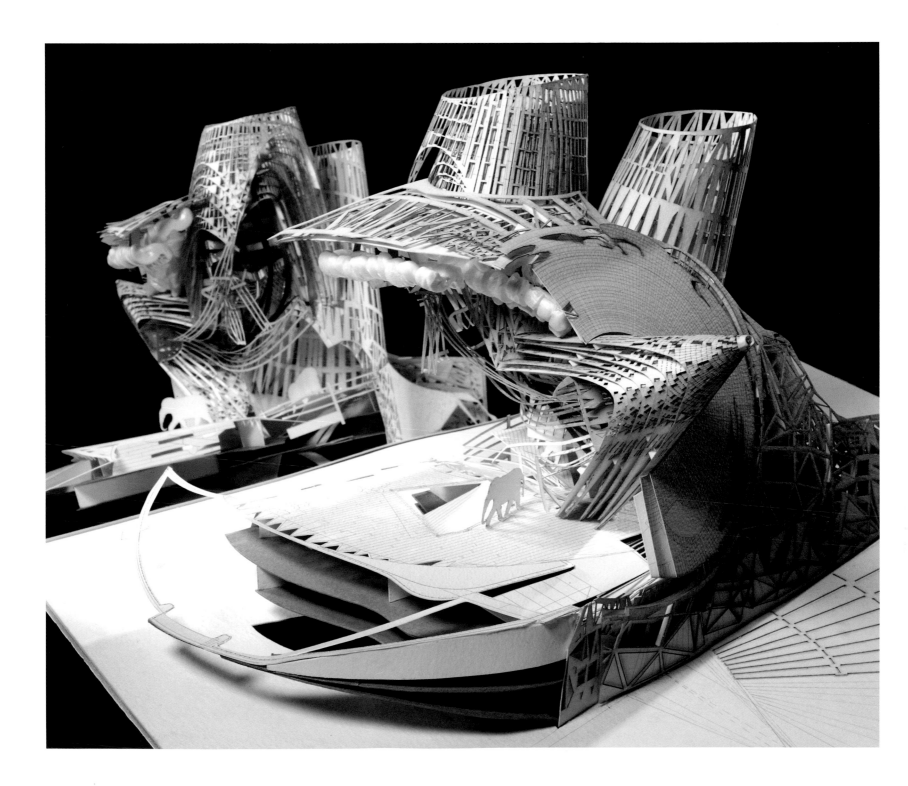

Section collage through south side of building.

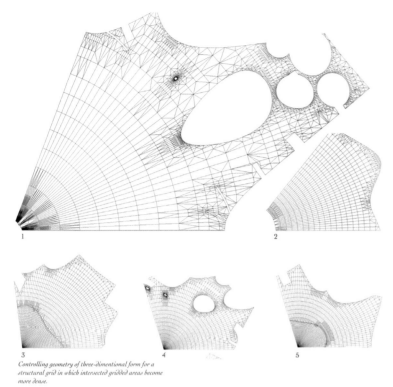

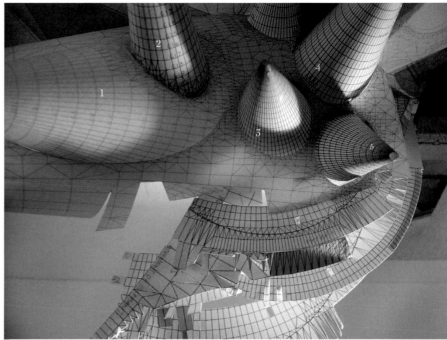

1 2

3 4 5

Controlling geometry of three-dimentional form for a structural grid in which intersected gridded areas become more dense.

Detail tracing paper model with its unfolded surfaces.

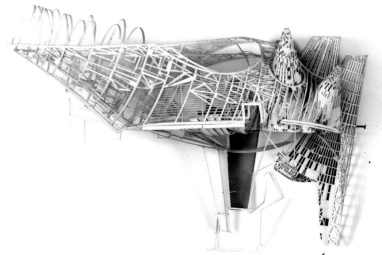

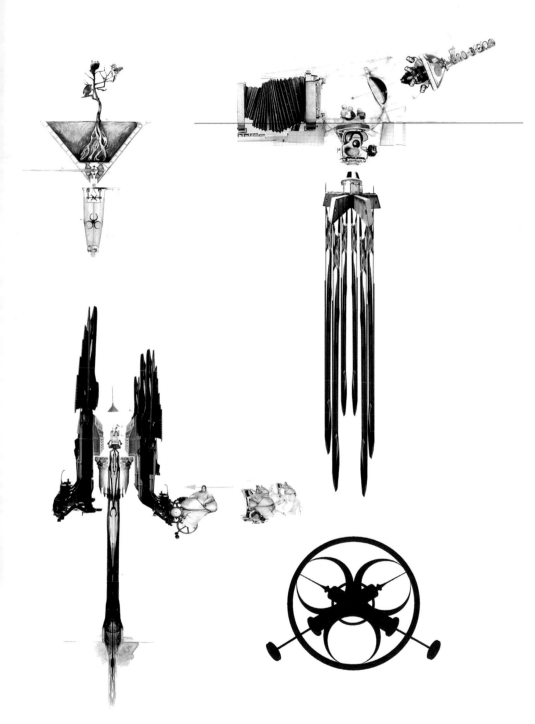

Ministry of Pestilence

Kate Davies
Diploma Architecture (2005)
Tutors: *Bob Sheil, Zoe Smith* and *Graeme Williamson*

This project imagines a mythical government building – the Ministry of Pestilence – as an allegorical fiction of the near future. It casts a satirical eye over the UK government and the politics of fear, post 9/11. A series of thwarted attempts at biological terrorism fill the newspapers, vaccines are stockpiled and the whole country is on red alert. The Ministry of Pestilence has been created to fight an invisible foe – an enemy among us – with biological weapons. This is warfare on the scale of the body, and everyone is a suspected 'carrier'. While the Intelligence Department scans the horizon for the wrong kind of wind, and Quarantine imprisons anyone who sneezes, business bosses wine and dine the minister, the press officers burn memos to keep warm, and the Bio-Labs develop their own deadly virus.

Mobile Appliances for the Hells Angels

Caspar Rodgers
Diploma Architecture (2007)
Tutors: *John Puttick*, *Peter Szczepaniak* and *Iain Borden*

Both the FBI in the United States and the Criminal Intelligence Service in Canada believe that motorcycle-riding members of the Hells Angels commonly carry out widespread violence and extortion, while also dealing in drugs and stolen goods. Many Hells Angels deny such accusations, and claim instead that they are simply a group of motorcycle enthusiasts who organise social events such as road trips, parties, rallies and even fund-raising occasions.

This project – part ironic, part fantastical, part real – provides a series of mobile appliance-architectures for the Hells Angels, such as a fuel rig, maintenance workshop and tattoo parlour, to help them pursue their transient and semi-mythic lifestyle. The design project is supported by a detailed sociological investigation into the constitution of the Hells Angels, presented in the form of a how-to 'Haynes' manual.

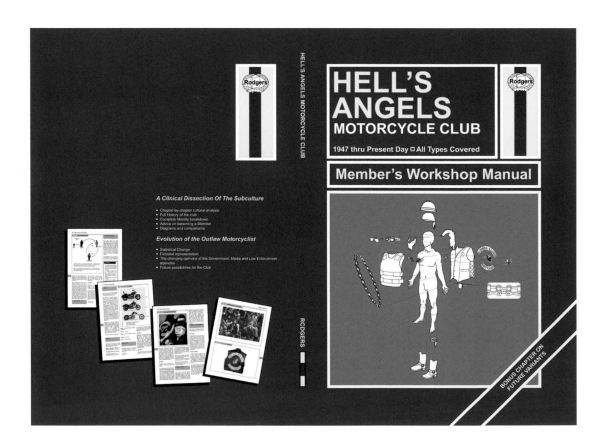

Nano-Prosthetics

Glen Tomlin
Diploma Architecture (2005)
Tutors: *Neil Spiller* and *Phil Watson*

The research underlying the 'Nano-Prosthetics' project explores myriad vectors and spaces which are never seen or appreciated, and which are generated as a side effect of the creation of a recognised masterpiece, in this case Picasso's *Les Demoiselles d'Avignon*. In the design project, nanotechnological devices are used as implants at an artist's wrist, elbow and shoulder. As the work was in progress, three other nested 'paintings' were generated. Simultaneously, such nanotechnological devices could also act as preventative medical sensors, sensing the health of the user's bone marrow, blood constitution, muscle fibre and nervous system.

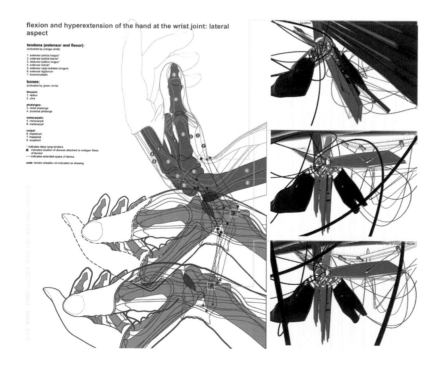

Narration

Jonathan Hill
and **Jane Rendell**

This two-sided text approaches architecture through narration and story-telling, processes that are both interpretative (that allow us to consider the plot, character, voice and tone of buildings) and generative (that propose the device of story-telling as a way of suggesting the design of programme, content and materialisation in architecture).

Narrative

The idea that Modernism has no history before the early 20th century is a myth, and historians have resorted to different periods to give it a past. As early as 1929, architectural historian Henry-Russell Hitchcock identified the origins of Modernism in the 18th-century Picturesque and Romantic movements.[1] But the desire to change society, not merely to reflect it, soon hardened into the denigration of past architectures and past lives.

Recognising Modernism's denial of its own history, American architect Robert Venturi's *Complexity and Contradiction in Architecture* (1966) was at the vanguard of Post-Modernism – but Post-Modernism was not necessarily new. In his essay 'Of the Standard of Taste' (1757), the Scottish philosopher David Hume writes that '[b]eauty is no quality in things themselves: it exists merely in the mind which contemplates them; and each mind perceives a different beauty'.[2] The 18th century endlessly lauded individual insight but acknowledged its uncertainty and changeability. Undoubtedly this was one of its attractions, fuelling the elusive search for the transient self. The highly self-conscious and meandering narration in the English novelist Laurence Sterne's *The Life and Opinions of Tristram Shandy, Gentleman* (1759–67) is a Post-Modernist text written some two hundred years before Post-Modernism. Sterne's complex visual and typographical devices — 'tripping us up as we read'[3] — ensure the reader's concentration and communicate when words cannot, calling attention to the limits of image and text. The narrator sets out to tell the story of his life but rarely gets beyond his conception, birth and early childhood, indicating that no text can fully encapsulate the complexity of a person. But Sterne's fractured narrative actually offers a more detailed, nuanced and honest portrait than a linear narrative. *Tristram Shandy* was influential and admired, notably by the English architect John Soane, who applied narration to his house and museum in Lincoln's Inn Fields between 1792 and 1837. The silent museum of today is quite unlike 12–14 Lincoln's Inn Fields in Soane's time, when workmen were ever-present. Remaining on site while three adjacent buildings were acquired, demolished and adjusted, Soane ruined as much as he built, continuing alterations until his death in 1837 at the age of 84, when his ever-changing narrative came to an end.

Narrative is unrewarding when it is didactic. The more suggestive narration of Sterne and Soane was revived in the French intellectual Roland Barthes' essay 'The Death of the Author' (1968), which proposes a writer aware of the creativity of the reader and, by implication, an architect aware of the creativity of the user.[4] Post-Modernism drew attention to concerns that were latent but suppressed in Modernism, allowing narration and narrative to be explicit design strategies once again. Since the 1980s, the denigration of Post-Modernism suggests that its concerns for meaning, narrative and history have been ignored. But we are all Post-Modernists now. Figurative, as well as abstract, architecture is a language once again. While misunderstandings are guaranteed, and may even be rewarding, architecture is a means to engage in discourses within the profession and beyond. In projects produced at the UCL Bartlett School of Architecture during the last 10 years, narratives of the past as well as the future have been ever-present. To cite but one example, darkly evocative and replete with typographical devices, Ben Clement's 'Bankrupts' Institute, Venice', has further relevance to Soane and Sterne because its starting point is William Hogarth's *A Rake's Progress* (1733–4), which Soane purchased in 1802, while Hogarth illustrated early editions of *Tristram Shandy* at Sterne's request. Inverting Hogarth's narrative and denying his didacticism, Clement suggests that bankruptcy can even be a gift, liberating the bankrupt from materialism and leading to self-reflection. In the 'Bankrupts' Institute', 'a rake's progress' is meant without irony.

Architecture-Writing

In pursuit of the development of a new way of telling stories in architectural practice, at the juncture of theory and design, and combining both drawing and writing, a number of Bartlett projects over the past 10 years have investigated various interconnected themes: first, an articulation of the interactive relationship between writing and designing; second, an exploration of the materiality of visio-spatial processes which combine written and drawn texts; third, a development of the particular spatial and architectural qualities of story-telling; fourth, a blending of personal and academic writing styles to develop multiple voices and different subject positions; fifth, an investigation of how physical journeys through architectural spaces work in dialogue with changes in psychic and emotional states; and, sixth, an examination of how responses to specific sites can pattern the form as well as the content of texts generating new genres for architectural writing based on letters, diaries, guidebooks, (auto)biographies and travelogues.

These various students' projects and texts in many cases draw on, but also extend, the research conducted in this area of architectural writing by literary critics and architectural designers and theorists – including many at the Bartlett itself. Outside of the school, for example, Mary Ann Caws's concept of 'architexture' is helpful here in allowing us to take texts, structures which are not buildings, as forms of architecture. A term that refers to the act of reading rather than writing, for Caws, architexture 'situates the text in the world of other texts', drawing attention to the surface and texture of the text as a form of construction.[5] Architecture-writings and site-writings expand this potential by performing their critical arguments through the creation of texts which are architecturally composed, interweaving critical and autobiographical voices, to produce hybrid artefacts with multiple subject positions.[6]

In the discipline of architecture itself, several writers have engaged with the potential of writing architecture. In *Atlas of Emotion*, Giuliana Bruno sets forth an aim that the form of the book she is writing will follow the design of the building in which she works,[7] while Katja Grillner has been exploring the possibilities for a writing that is architectural, by, for example, situating herself as a subject in a landscape, among those she writes about.[8] Karen Bermann's reflection on Anne Frank's diary describes the spaces provided by writing while hiding as a 'mobile homeland', articulated by a hybrid text fashioned through spatial details and conditions.[9] But perhaps the written projects of architect and critic Jennifer Bloomer have been the most influential in their attempt to build architecture. Spatially structured, Bloomer's texts operate metaphorically to explore imaginative narratives and employ metonymic devices to bring the non-appropriate into architecture. For Bloomer, different modes of writing construct architecture through the intimate and personal, through sensual rather than purely visual stimulation.[10]

At the Bartlett, both undergraduate and graduate students alike explore the relationship between architecture and other disciplines – feminist theory and architectural history, fine art and architectural design, architecture and writing – and bring processes from fine art practice and architectural design to inform the production of site-specific writing. Besides design work, the texts produced are often designed constructions – spatial in their form and architectonic in their structure. See for example the Diploma Architecture work of students Daniel Brady, Lucy Leonard, Fiona Sheppard and Zoe Quick, where concepts are generated, spaces are imagined, and artefacts emerge as constellations of images, lines and words. In the MA Architectural History, a brief to produce a piece of 'site-specific writing' encourages the students to new ways of composing texts that bring spatial qualities of sites into the production of the writing, generating guidebooks, websites, diaries and textual objects, as in the work of Sophie Handler.[11]

In both the MPhil/PhD Architectural History and Theory and the MPhil/PhD Architectural Design programmes, students explore the creative potential of critical writing as a form of architectural practice, sometimes explicating historiographic ideas through different writing genres, weaving intimate personal narratives and more academically poised arguments, as in the research of Lilian Chee, and in other cases, developing practice-led research through the production of site-specific texts – poetic installations and performative criticism.

References
1 Henry-Russell Hitchcock, *Modern Architecture: Romanticism and Regeneration*, Hacker Art Books (New York), 1970, p 12.
2 David Hume, 'Of the Standard of Taste', Stephen Copley and Andrew Edgar (eds), *Selected Essays*, Oxford University Press (Oxford), 1993, pp 136–7.
3 William V Holtz, Image and Immortality: a Study of 'Tristram Shandy', Brown University Press (Providence), 1970, p 88.
4 Roland Barthes, 'The Death of the Author', *Image-Music-Text*, Flamingo (London), 1977, p 148.
5 Mary Ann Caws, *A Metapoetics of the Passage: Architextures in Surrealism and After*, University Press of New England (Hanover and London), 1981, p xiv.
6 Jane Rendell, 'Architecture-Writing', Jane Rendell (ed), *Critical Architecture*, special issue of the *Journal of Architecture*, v 10, n 3 (June 2005), pp 255–64; Jane Rendell, 'Site-Writing: Enigma and Embellishment', Jane Rendell, Jonathan Hill, Murray Fraser and Mark Dorrian (eds), *Critical Architecture*, Routledge (London), 2007; and Jane Rendell, *Site-Writing: the Architecture of Art Criticism*, IB Tauris (London), forthcoming.
7 Giuliana Bruno, *Atlas of Emotion: Journeys in Art, Architecture and Film*, Verso (London), 2002. p 112
8 Katja Grillner, 'Writing and Landscape – Setting Scenes for Critical Reflection', Jonathan Hill (ed), *Opposites Attract*, special issue of *The Journal of Architecture*, v 8, n 2 (2003), pp 239–49; and Katja Grillner, *Ramble, Linger and Gaze: Dialogues from the Landscape Garden*, Axl Books (Stockholm), 2000.
9 Karen Bermann, 'The House Behind', Heidi J Nast and Steve Pile (eds), *Places Through the Body*, Routledge (London), 1998, pp 165–80.
10 Jennifer Bloomer, 'Big Jugs', Arthur Kroker and Marilouise Kroker (eds), *The Hysterical Male: New Feminist Theory*, Macmillan Education (London), 1991, pp 13–27; and Jennifer Bloomer, *Architecture and the Text: the (S)crypts of Joyce and Piranesi*, Yale University Press (New Haven and London), 1993.
11 Sophie Handler's project is a deliberate re-working of Jane Rendell, 'Doing it, (Un)Doing it, (Over)Doing it Yourself: Rhetorics of Architectural Abuse', Jonathan Hill (ed), *Occupying Architecture*, Routledge (London), 1998, pp 229–46.

National Park of the Interior

John Norman
Diploma Architecture (2006)
Tutors: *Simon Herron* and *Susanne Isa*

The 'National Park of the Interior' explores the national park as a representational model and as a home for the photographer Ansel Adams. As visitors move through the house, they experience changing scales of observation within the optical and scalar thresholds. The house allows you to discover the park within the house, and the house within the park. Throughout the project there is an interest in the relationship between the photograph and the architectural representation. These twin points of view are shown through corresponding drawings for each method of representation.

Observatory and Ticket Office, Foro Romano, Rome

Ben Cowd
Diploma Architecture (2007)
Tutors: *Marjan Colletti* and *Marcos Cruz*

Inspired by cosmic diagrams of ancient civilisations, the project focuses on the theme of cosmology and sacred space. Mapping the paths and cycles of the sun and stars, contoured surfaces can be read as astronomical clocks and calendars: steps representing days and months, stones representing minutes, and lines attributed to seconds. The cartography of these studies is generated by a series of recessed laser-cut drawings and models. The final proposal of a public observatory and ticket office, placed in the complex historic context of the Foro Romano, interprets the formal intricacy, density and diversity of patterns found among the ruins.

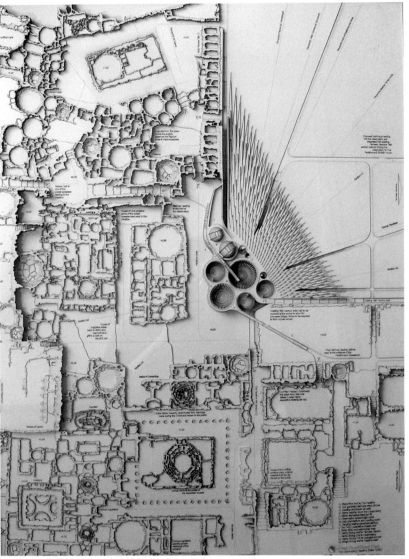

One Million Square Feet of Love

Nicholas Henderson
Diploma Architecture (2004)
Tutor: *Nic Clear*

'One Million Square Feet of Love: a Complete Do-It-Yourself Manual' is set in the Stanley Dock Tobacco Warehouse in Liverpool. The project uses film and graphics to propose a gradual transformation of the warehouse into an anarcho-syndicalist organisation. Undaunted by the huge scale of the building, Henderson sets out a clear 20-year plan where the architecture is gradually overtaken and reconstructed by its inhabitants. The film's CAD-style motion graphics, which are incorporated into an accompanying written thesis, are presented as a cross between a revolutionary manifesto and a DIY manual. Predicated on visionary ideals of figures ranging from Charles Fourier to Constant to Lebbeus Woods, the project pays homage to the collective values of Henderson's home town, Liverpool.

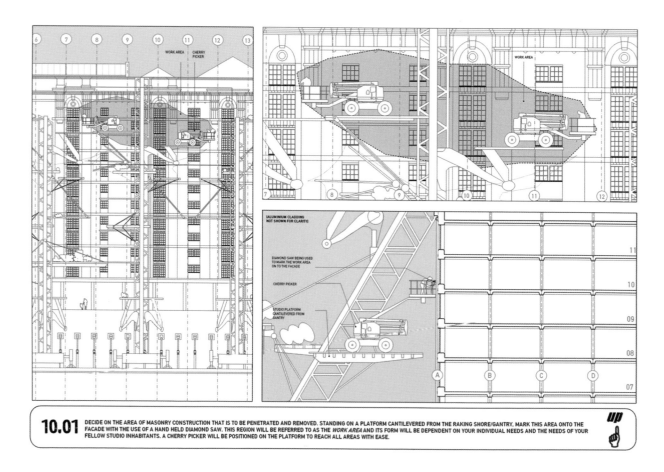

10.01 DECIDE ON THE AREA OF MASONRY CONSTRUCTION THAT IS TO BE PENETRATED AND REMOVED. STANDING ON A PLATFORM CANTILEVERED FROM THE RAKING SHORE/GANTRY, MARK THIS AREA ONTO THE FACADE WITH THE USE OF A HAND HELD DIAMOND SAW. THIS REGION WILL BE REFERRED TO AS THE *WORK AREA* AND ITS FORM WILL BE DEPENDENT ON YOUR INDIVIDUAL NEEDS AND THE NEEDS OF YOUR FELLOW STUDIO INHABITANTS. A CHERRY PICKER WILL BE POSITIONED ON THE PLATFORM TO REACH ALL AREAS WITH EASE.

Opera House, Gibraltar

Harriet Lee
BSc Architecture (2003)
Tutors: *Laura Allen* and *Mark Smout*

Clinging perilously to Mediterranean cliffs, the 'Opera House' marries an adventurous structural solution with acoustic devices that are created by the form of the building and its relationship with the supporting rocks.

The scheme serves both Gibraltar's local community, and holidaymakers who tour on cruise ships through the Straits of Gibraltar. It functions as a visual and acoustic conduit, borrowing reflective surfaces from surrounding terrain to project performances out to sea, thus erasing the boundary between the internal and external through the exchange of sight and sound. Peripheral spaces provide enhanced environmental acoustics, with aural snapshots being released from within the hidden confines of dressing rooms and rehearsal spaces. The delicate carapace, from which the diva emerges, is formed from porcelain and bronze to both radiate and reflect light.

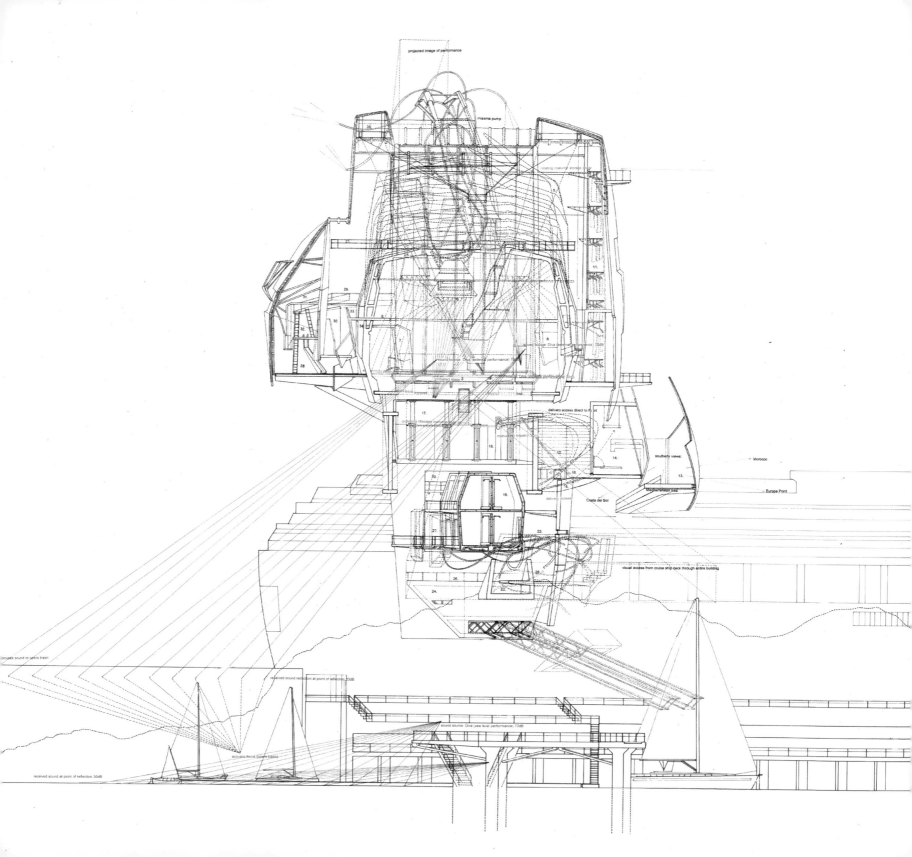

projected image of performance

miasma pump

rotating costume storage

sound source: Diva (internal performance) 70dB

delivery access direct to fly pit

southerly views: Morocco

Mediterranean Sea

Costa del Sol   Europe Point

visual access from cruise ship deck through entire building

focuses sound to opera basin

received sound reflection at point of reflection 70dB

sound source: Diva (sea level performance) 70dB

acoustic focus (opera basin)

received sound at point of reflection 30dB

Opium Refinery, London

Owen Jones
Diploma Architecture (2008)
Tutors: *Peter Culley* and *Christine Hawley*

This project addresses the contemporary need of the NHS to find alternative legal sources of opium from which pain-killing morphine can be extracted. Opium poppies are first grown on isolated security rafts at the mouth of the Thames Estuary, and then floated to the refinery on a waterfront site beside St Thomas' Hospital in central London. Here, the plants are systematically harvested, processed and refined.

The architectural language reflects the processes required for extracting and drying opium sap, and the chemical process of refining and purifying, so the building has the quality of a highly polished machine. But it also has another function, to act as a reminder of London's dirtier history as a site of opium consumption in the 18th century and its oft-forgotten participation in the illicit opium trade in 19th-century China. The project thus depicts a substance that is not only a critical component of the modern medical armoury but also the path to drug-addicted destruction. Within this polished sculptural shell lies a sparkling, clinical interior and the dark corridors of history.

Palais Idéal

Bastian Glassner
MArch Architecture (2001)
Tutor: *Nic Clear*

'Palais Idéal' consists of a sequence of animated 'digital paintings' or abstract digital landscapes. Acting as a contemporary bricoleur, images are culled from a variety of 'actual' sources, scanned objects and manipulated photographs. Combined with images produced within a digital environment, the whole selection is then morphed within the CGI film environment. This film-based project creates a strange, sensuous, coalescing landscape of stylistic excess, the visual power of which is further enhanced by a haunting soundtrack. It represents a highly innovative and technical tour de force, and is named in honour of the iconic structure created by Ferdinand Cheval in Hauterives.

Parliament Building, Hong Kong

Andrew Stanforth
Diploma Architecture (2003)
Tutors: *Christine Hawley* and *cj Lim*

The whole area of Hong Kong – the Island, Kowloon and the New Territories – is divided into sections akin to parliamentary wards, each of which has easy access to water. In this project, constituency offices are located in these wards, floating on the waterfront. Each office is a mobile capsule containing all the essentials for administration, consultation and communication. Its location is convenient and accessible, providing residents with a level of service that is impossible under the existing system. Once the parliamentary call is made, all MPs use their water-mobile capsules to converge on the parliamentary core, located within an artificially created harbour on Hong Kong Island. This core is a debating chamber that is used for public events throughout the year, but every six weeks – when the constituency capsules dock onto the core infrastructure – the combined structure provides a parliament building equipped for representation at the highest level.

Patent Office and Archive, London

Luke Chandresinghe
Diploma Architecture (2006)
Tutors: *Simon Herron* and *Susanne Isa*

This beautiful project is for a depository for patents held in a protected stasis for 20 years, following a rigorous process of application, inspection-verification, final granting and protection. It deploys a post-industrial machine aesthetic, created from collaged assemblies that are dismantled, reassembled, restructured and recomposed. As with patent drawings, the complete function remains somewhat elusive, it is strictly limited, with information only glimpsed. No single view or patent reveals the entire design.

This is a monument to the production of things, seen as an arcane industrialised process of intellectual property. Processed ideas are held in giant vortex fields, and then ejected tangentially outward through an exfoliating skin, surrounded by a market-driven hinterland trading in second-hand ideas.

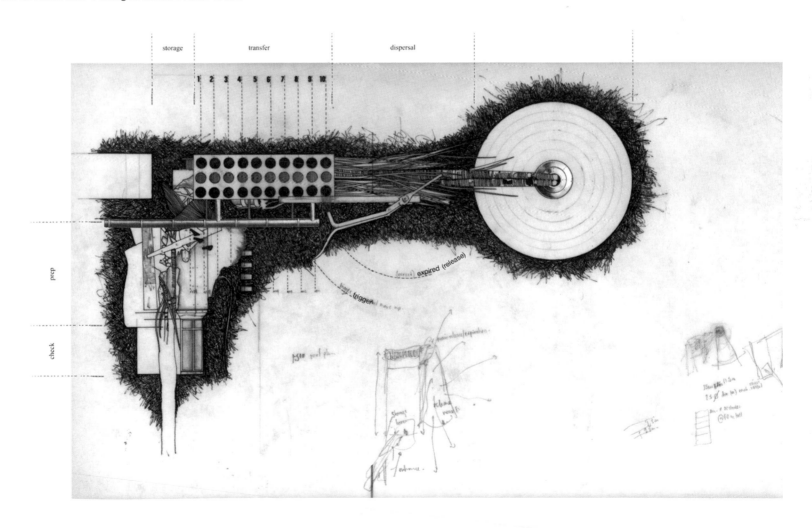

Perceptual Observatory, Greenwich

Steve Westcott
Diploma Architecture (2007)
Tutors: *Niall McLaughlin* and *Yeoryia Manolopoulou*

The new 'Perceptual Observatory' is a reformulation of the earliest Observatory within Greenwich, Flamsteed House. It is inspired by the principles of Kurt Schwitters' *Merzbau* and by investigations generated by Herman Melville's *Moby Dick*.

The project investigates both the process of collection as a facilitator of knowledge, and architecture's role in enhancing perceptual experience. Studies of visual perception, the landscape and history of the Greenwich Observatory are turned into a complex of rooms, courtyards, views and towers, all woven around a new open-air matrix replacing the original Octagon Room. The project is a journey in time, a remembered room, a machine for looking, a place for architectural enquiry and drawing, and a site for allegory and myths.

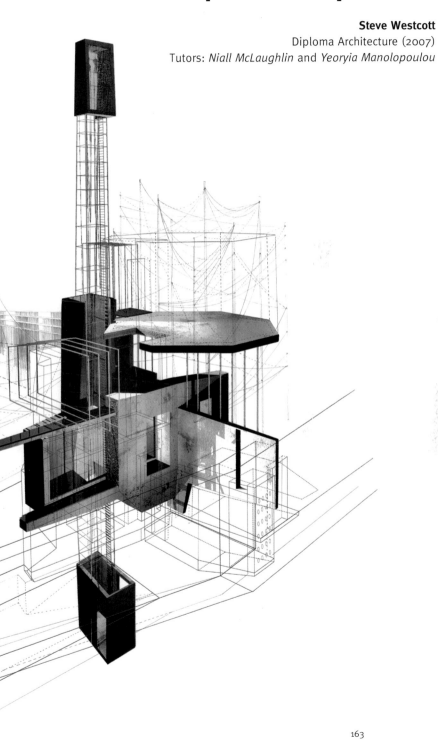

Ruairi Glynn
Diploma Architecture (2008)
Tutors: *Phil Ayres*, *Stephen Gage* and *James O'Leary*

Architecture is differentiated from building in that it induces sensations of delight and wonder in its observers. Where does this delight or wonder reside? According to Heinz Von Foerster's definition, a work of architecture is the physical embodiment of a trivial machine (a constructed construct). The process of constructing such a machine for the first time, however, is not trivial, and can induce sensations of delight. This applies both to the person who designs the machine (the architect) and to the observer who reconstructs it in her or his own understanding. In this installation, a constantly evolving community of 'Dancers' improvises performances and evaluates the facial reactions of people observing them. Using genetic algorithms, they begin to learn how best to please their audiences.

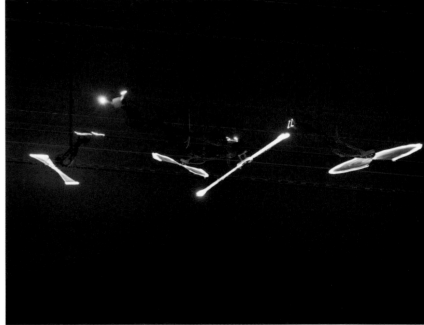

Performed City

Abigail Yeates
Diploma Architecture (2005)
Tutor: *Nic Clear*

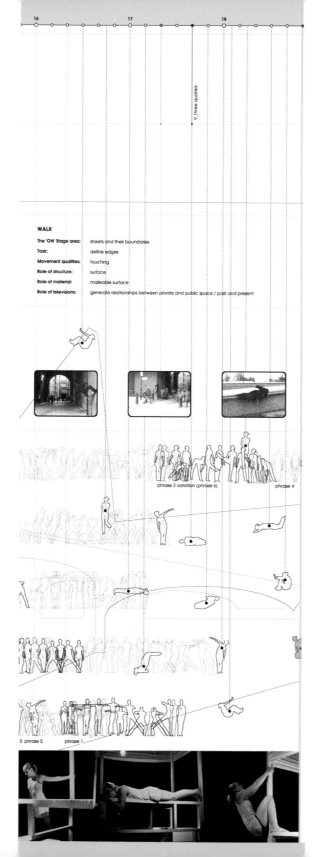

This project is a collaboration between architecture student Abigail Yeates and dancer choreographer Natasha Mansfield-Osborne. Using as a starting point Yeates's graphics that map out a journey through the city, the pair work between drawings and dance, playing with the idea of adapting each other's notation system. The culmination is a 30-minute performance, integrating the graphic process and dance, as well as installation and film narrative. The performance uses the narrative device of the journey of a day to structure the movement sequences. This collaboration between designer and dancer creates a synthesis between the spatial representations of architecture and the spatial practices of dance and theatre. The installation designed by Yeates is a performed drawing, but it is a drawing of a performance by a body in space and time, and one that actively embraces the possibility of misreading.

Perfumery and Exercise Facility

Tom Holberton
Diploma Architecture (2005)
Tutor: *Christine Hawley*

The project attenuates a well-trodden commuter path between the River Thames and Temple Garden into a running track, which in turn looks down upon a gym, sunk below ground level. A discrete perfumery is also inserted, and the manufacture of oil and essence become a critical part of the architectural vocabulary. This function makes an ironic reference to the site, the location of London's first main sewer. Technical inventiveness permeates the project. The roof is a sequence of glass receptacles, filling and emptying according to the chemical processes taking place elsewhere. The external facade is a glistening wall of changing hue.

Pie Shop, Bloomsbury, London

Ian Laurence, Karl Normanton and **Frances Taylor**
Diploma Architecture (2005)
Tutors: *Phil Ayres, Stephen Gage, Usman Haque* and *Neil Spiller*

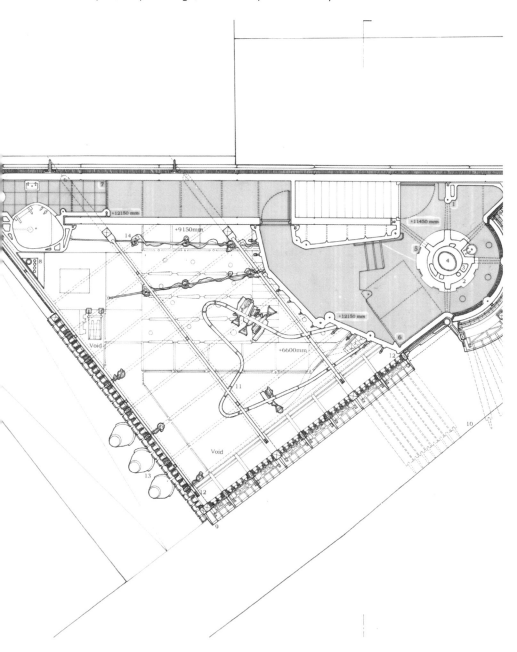

This impressively detailed and resolved project – richly informed by additional technical advice and criticism from Buro Happold, Kate Crawford, Michael Hadi, Ron Packman, John Spaans and Simon Goode – encompasses the design of everything from a menu to architecture.

Conceived as a small stage set, the programme explores, both functionally and spatially, the theatre inherent in the retail catering industry. The business is owned and run by a retired master baker who lives on the premises. He is passionate about pies. Essentially the shop is a daytime establishment, serving breakfast and lunch, with evening events and functions by arrangement. A takeaway service is provided on the ground floor. The owner employs students from the dance school opposite the site.

The major element is an articulated oven stack, which operates as a spatial device and as a mechanism for environmental control through a double-flue system. A thick-crusted element, it retains and radiates its collected heat and remains cool in the summer. The oven distends vertically through the building, forming warm or cool (depending on the time of year) coffered observation spaces for the public. These spaces are used by the dance students to stretch, limber up or cool down. A whiff of voyeurism can be sensed in the sight-lines of the design.

A series of mechanical devices, each with their own specific attributes, adds to the theatre of production and consumption. From the kitchen to the stalls, the automated forms of servery and the dance students animate the set in a carefully choreographed service. A dynamic facade that mediates daylight and acts as a rain screen operates as a two-way backdrop for both customers and the passers-by on the street outside.

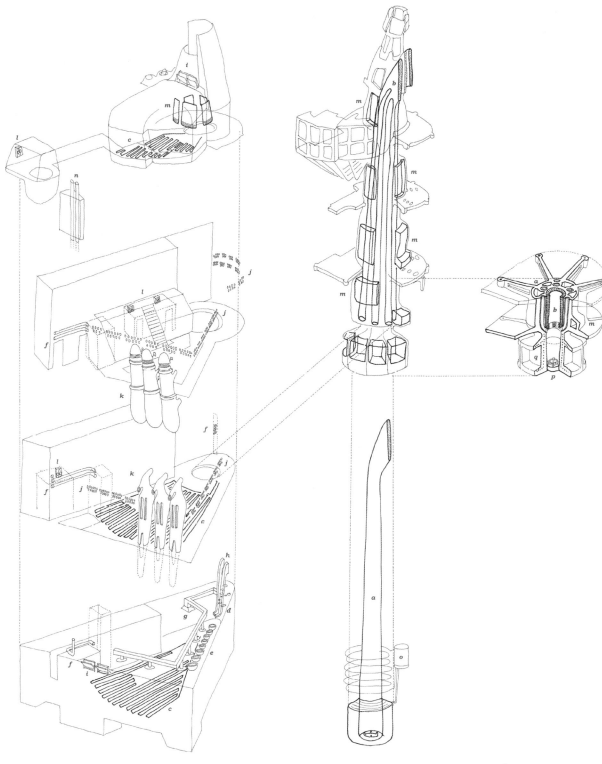

Bloomsbury Pie Shop:
Heating, Cooling and Ventilation

a Condensing flue
b Non-condensing flue
c Under floor heating
d Plant room smoke vents
e Glass 'basin' emergency smoke vents
f Lobby smoke vent
g Kitchen extraction
h Oven air intake
i Openable window
j Pie dish window vents
k Heat exchanger ventialtion alembics
l Wet area mechanical extraction
m Ovenstack warm panel space heater
n Riser stack vent
o Hot water heating
p Gas ring
q Oven

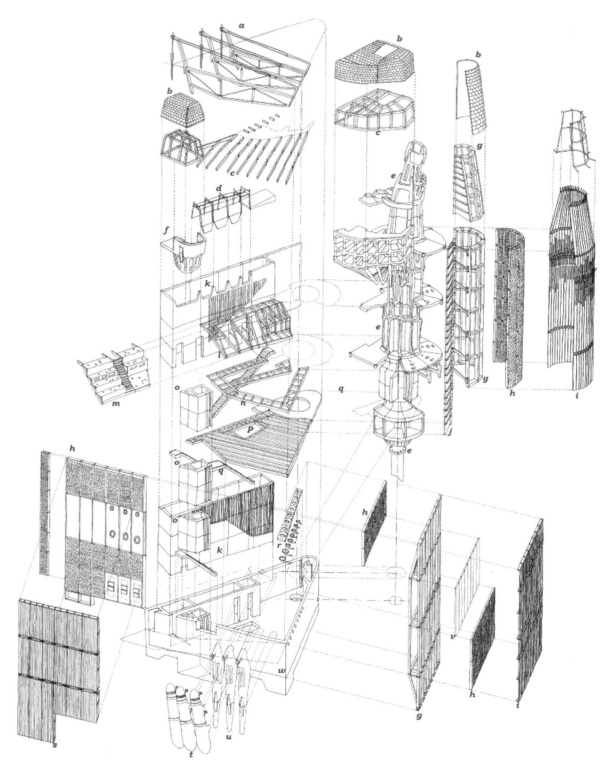

Bloomsbury Pie Shop:
Construction Elements

a Glulam roof trusses
b Shingle roof tiles
c Roof frame
d Core top/ bathroom corridor
e Ferrocement oven stack/ accommodation
f Ferrocement bathroom
g External façade primary structure
h Façade pie dish window cladding panels
i Ipe slat folding rainscreen
j Steel hinge
k Concrete stair core
l Paralam stalls structure
m Plywood stalls
n Circulation gantry structure
o Concrete lift core
p Upper ground/ takeaway level floor
q Stairs to stalls level
r Glass 'basin' drainage features
s Ipe fixed rainscreen cladding
t Ventilation alembics
u Storage silos
v Stalls level glazed façade
w Caltite concrete lower ground floor

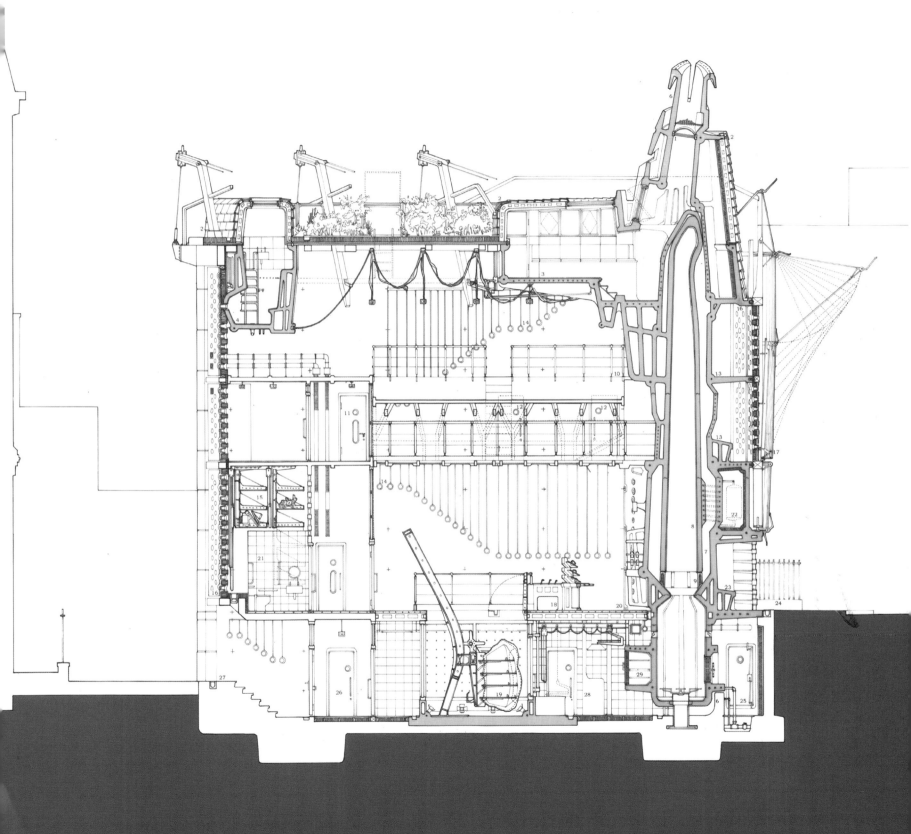

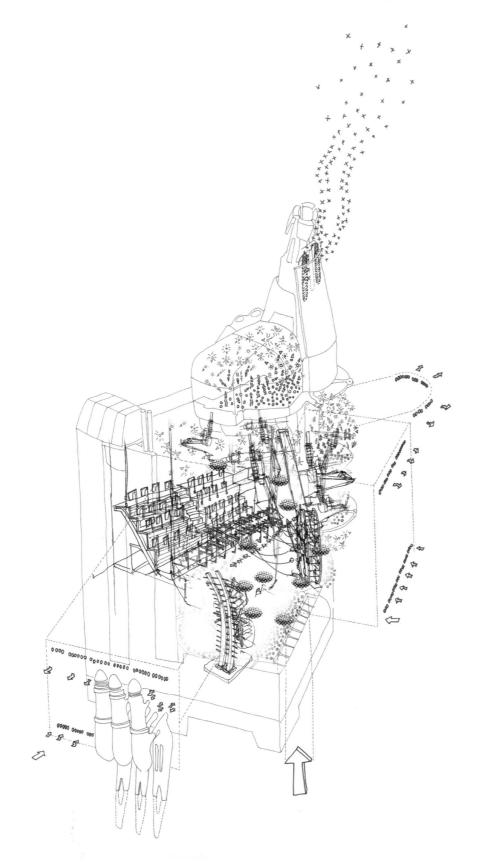

Bloomsbury Pie Shop:
Construction Elements

a Glulam roof trusses
b Shingle roof tiles
c Roof frame
d Core top/ bathroom corridor
e Ferrocement oven stack/ accommodation
f Ferrocement bathroom
g External façade primary structure
h Façade pie dish window cladding panels
i Ipe slat folding rainscreen
j Steel hinge
k Concrete stair core
l Paralam stalls structure
m Plywood stalls
n Circulation gantry structure
o Concrete lift core
p Upper ground/ takeaway level floor
q Stairs to stalls level
r Glass 'basin' drainage features
s Ipe fixed rainscreen cladding
t Ventilation alembics
u Storage silos
v Stalls level glazed façade
w Caltite concrete lower ground floor

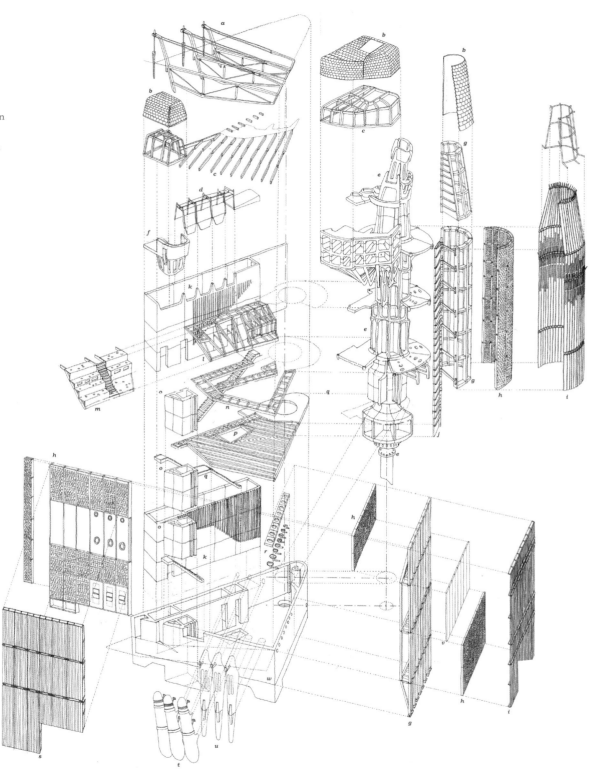

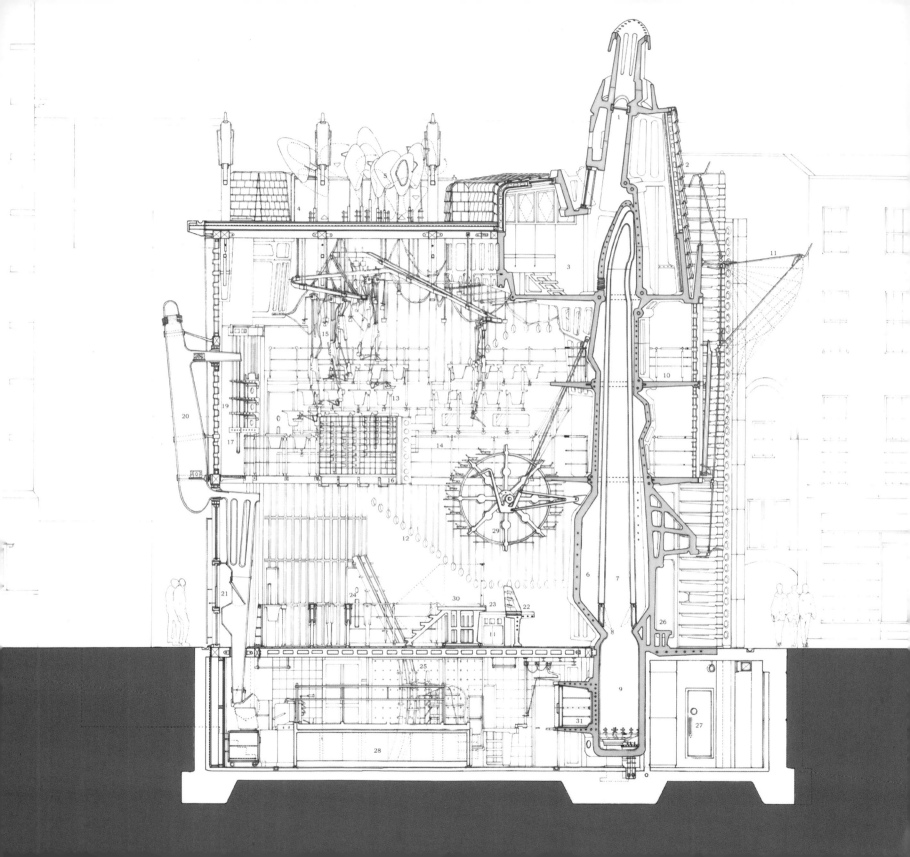

Pilgrimage Chapel, Rome

Jay Williams
Diploma Architecture (2007)
Tutors: *Marjan Colletti* and *Marcos Cruz*

The project proposes a new pilgrimage chapel in the Domitilla catacombs on the outskirts of Rome. Various ritualistic pilgrimage routes and tourist paths interlock and spiral downwards, creating new access to the catacombs. Intersecting walls, ramps and domes form open spaces for celebration. Hidden pockets embed confessionals, chapels and altars, as well as services for the rites of baptism, confession and prayer. An array of complex circulation systems creates mysterious and emotionally-loaded inner spaces for interior projections, religious performances and perspectival illusions.

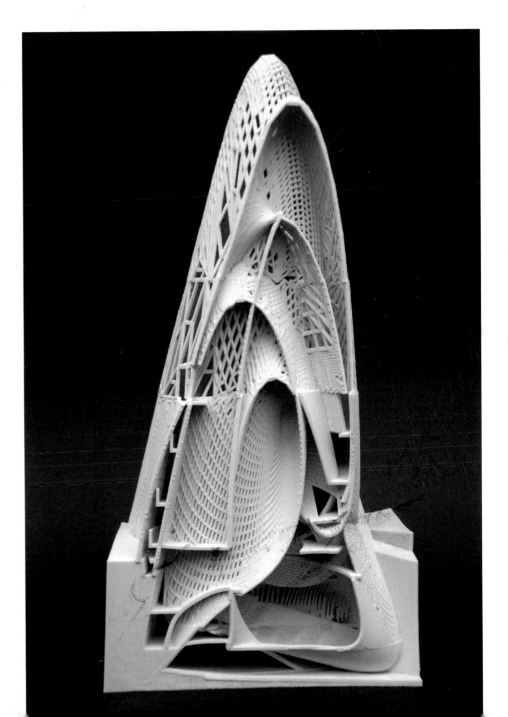

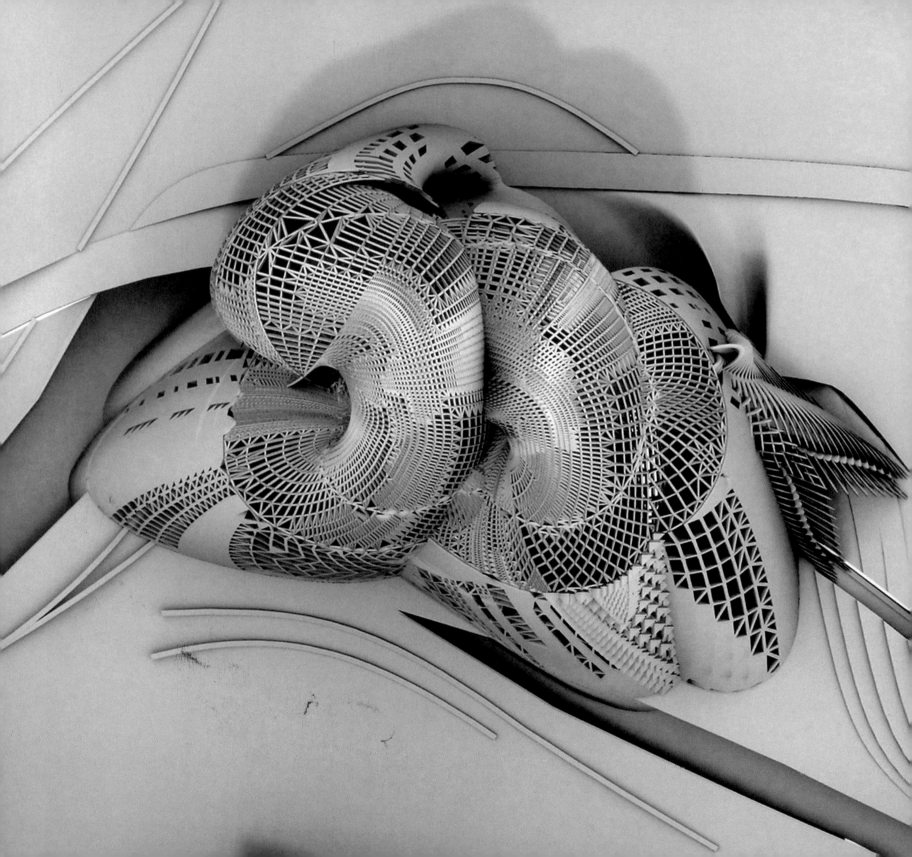

Cynthia Leung
Diploma Architecture (2006)
Tutors: *Bernd Felsinger* and *cj Lim*

The building is a place for women travellers, for which the project narrative stems from The *Wizard of Oz*, and in particular from Dorothy's ruby shoes. Expressions of femininity are an important part of the scheme: delicate smells of jasmine impregnate the air, while the clicking of high heel shoes on the bronze paving prompts fine mist to burst from the ground. These ephemeral spaces softly hover above the landscape. This unique setting facilitates dialogue, contemplation and entices women to travel. People exchange and recount their stories while sipping Chinese tea. Planting is artificial, and these floral motifs create a decorative blanket floating above the landscape.

Process

Colin Fournier and **Christine Hawley**

The journey that transforms a fragmentary initial concept into a functioning physical space has a broadly understood path. The process of creating a minimal mark that then acquires layers of information, which in turn are modified and manipulated through a series of iterations, is what we commonly think of as the design process. Within this sequence of steps, the idiosyncrasies of the individual, and the distracting conversations, can be expected and encouraged to disrupt what appears at first to be a clear sequential process and lead to innovative creative leaps and unpredictable outcomes.

In parallel with the pedagogical search for order, clarity and focus, there is an essential part of the studio discussion that deliberately challenges the fundamental understanding of occupied space, and instead explores more tentative and sometimes more obscure ideas, philosophical concepts and primary principles. In the commercial office, client aspiration, economic necessity, sometimes political directives and always legislative demands, will play a large and sometimes dominating role in the design and production of a building. But the academic studio environment offers an opportunity to suggest that the designer's role is to create wider horizons, raise radical aspirations and, through ingenuity, produce truly effective, and possibly hitherto unimagined, solutions. This is, of course, an idealised position and, cynically, everyone knows how difficult it is to create such a situation in reality. However, the academic preparation that students undertake should offer the opportunity to think far beyond obvious narrative, to speculate about the future and to take an intellectual proposition beyond its logical boundaries and customary pragmatic constraints. An essential part of the studio exercises should be the tentative exploration of the unknown and the radical demonstration of the 'extreme'.

To provoke such explorations, preliminary studio exercises focus on thematic issues and conceptual challenges shared across the group of students. They are asked to analyse and critique a range of ideas relating to a specific type of spatial occupation (such as the hotel room, the theatre space, the workplace); the nature of physical presence (land, water, edge, climate); contemporary issues (such as biomimetics, ecological sustainability or the impact of new communication technologies on architecture) or to explain the dynamics of a particular human behaviour and social activity (such as commerce, exchange, work, leisure); as well as emotions (fear, alienation, anxiety, surprise, pleasure). These themes are not attached to prescriptive architectural briefs; they demand an examination at a fundamental level. So, for example, it is understood that one must look critically at the nature of the activity, at the occupation and the influence of a particular cultural milieu, ideology or scientific paradigm, as well as at the physical environmental context.

At the core of these exercises is the need to understand fundamental characteristics, whether they be measurable in a technical sense (which they are often not), or whether they can be described through subjective narrative. The latter works smoothly when the characteristics are commonly shared and understood. However, the more interesting evaluation may arise from a highly idiosyncratic interpretation – and the challenge in this case is to substantiate any personal observation to a point where there is a collective understanding of the premise and of the intent.

To make a literal and articulated observation is at the core of any subsequent design development. These observations must be translated in to a graphic language and then further into physical form. The process of translation is multi-faceted; from narrative to figurative, often containing redundant or abandoned exercises, occasionally it can produce ideas that are a by-product and more intrinsically valuable to the generating theme. These ideas, which are at the heart of the concept, must be transposed into a physical artefact, which in turn accurately reflects the original thinking. Developing from these models are observations that give the original concept more depth and dimension and, in addition, allow for the unexpected intrusion of tangential themes that add new layers and complexity to the idea. The analysis may demonstrate the sensuality of material composition; if the model needs to be dynamic, it should demonstrably work. A suggestion about inhabited space is perhaps the most important outcome of this exercise, but with it come suggestions about materiality, qualities of light, the passage of time, dynamic change, iconography, ambiguity, seduction, desire, emotion – qualities that rarely feature in the traditional functional and commercial brief.

During this process, the architectural language becomes gradually embedded, first in the early explorations, then in the design drawings and the models. This is ultimately brought together with the necessary demands for functionality and occupation. The many layers of information necessary to allow a piece of architecture to emerge, the manipulation of information and often the rejection of lines of enquiry, are all a necessary part of this process. The most acute point comes when the overarching ideas, the principles, hitherto expressed only as abstract forms, need to accommodate a functional brief without losing the original radicality of intent. The challenge is that the poetics of the abstract run the risk, if one is not careful, of becoming subsumed under any one or all of the practical considerations. It is at this point that critical decisions are taken and that design talent has to manifest itself. The formal and acknowledged requirements of an architectural space must be questioned, the standard orthogonal relationships need to be reconsidered; the relationship between the occupant and volumetric space must be reassessed. There has to be a series of critical decisions in response to the question of whether the status quo of standardised responses is appropriate to support the central thesis. The process of negotiation critical in that judgement is used to decide what orthodoxies remain and what do not. This process is iterative and often tangential. Oblique avenues are explored to either justify and reinforce a decision, or to expel it for good. Through dialogue, negotiation, iteration and the slow accumulation of information and decision-making, the spatial proposition eventually emerges as a multi-layered palimpsest.

Prosthetic Mythologies

Kate Davies and **Emmanuel Vercruysse**
MArch Architecture (2007)
Tutors: *Bob Sheil* and *Graeme Williamson*

Kielder is a manufactured forest in Northumbria devoid of the history of mythology coursing through the ancient Boreal zones. It is a prosthetic landscape, a graft, a dark internal wilderness of quiet psychological exposure. 'Prosthetic Mythologies' is an automated performance for Kielder. A colony of sculptural and sonic automata resides deep in the forest. They are crepuscular – activated only by low light. Their combined response to the specific light conditions of their individual sites forms a rhythmic composition in two parts: The Vespertine (dusk) and The Matinal (dawn). During dusk, each piece hammers out its private rhythm, those deeper in the forest activating first. The tempo of each rhythm increases as light falls, and it builds to a climax of rhythmic layers falling in and out of step with each other, evoking a feverish ritual. Then one by one they fall silent, awaiting dawn.

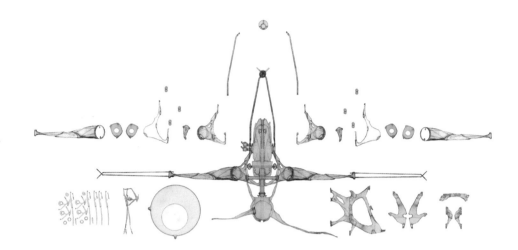

Reflexive Lagoon

This scheme is located in the canals and lagoon of Venice. The proposition rejoices in the natural phenomenology of the area, in Venice's tides, silt, gentle decomposition and winds. A series of sensors and drivers constantly react, quivering and activating subtle architectural conversations. High-tech reeds mix realities, memories and sensations.

Irini Androutsopoulou
MArch Architectural Design (2006)
Tutor: *Stuart Munro*

Salt Marsh's apparatus recreating the surface of the lagoon
Perspective View

Remote Prosthetics

Michael Wihart
MArch Architectural Design (2005)
Tutor: *Phil Watson*

The work is part of the creation of a series of 'Soft Architectural Machines'. Architecture is slowly coming to terms with the impact of advanced technology. Here, the project explores the ecologies of small machines that are made of nanotechnological, mechanical and biotechnological elements, and how these ecologies might be able to swarm together to create architectural space. The project also explores certain conditions of speed, and particularly how these spaces might reconfigure (slowly) over time.

Resonant Observatory, UCL

Tim Barwell
Diploma Architecture (2007)
Tutors: *Bob Sheil* and *Graeme Williamson*

The site is set within the quadrangle of UCL's main campus – a redundant observatory, now unused as the night sky has been long obscured by London's artificial radiance. So what might this observatory observe closer to the ground, and what might it observe of things we can't see? After many iterations testing, for example, humidity, sunlight, user behaviour, material behaviour, air movement, the final ambient 'Resonant Observatory' stands on the centrepoint of the internal observatory space. Its 'leaves' are activated by a cluster of orchid-like wax-filled thermo pumps located on the external crown of the dome. Connected by an array of piano wire to these pumps, the leaves expand and contract 'in tune' with the external ambient temperature. Passers-by may strike the wires and play the musical note of that instant.

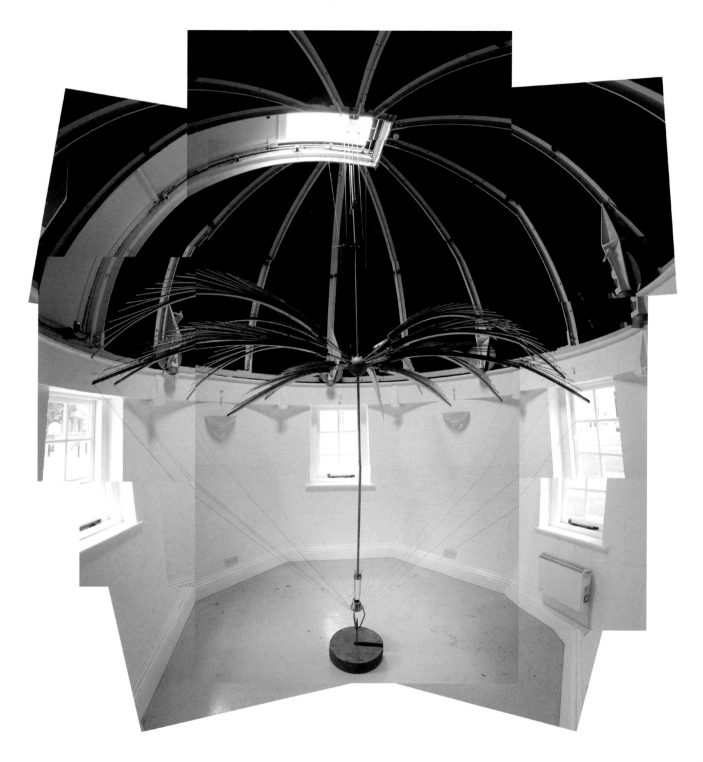

Retirement Home, Newcastle-upon-Tyne

Luke Pearson
BSc Architecture (2005)
Tutors: *Laura Allen* and *Mark Smout*

Set in Newcastle's Bigg Market, the project is a witty yet sensitive retirement home for elderly fishermen, and a working men's club, responding to local problems of redundancy and an ageing population.

As a reflection of the separation and torpor of this unique society, the scheme uses the notion of the ship in an architectural context, creating an ersatz environment which interacts with the city around it as if it were a dry docked vessel. Artificial horizons present both the deck and the air space of Newcastle as a pair of seas, viewed as if from the crow's nest. By day, it is visible as a series of profiles and devices. At night, the deck becomes a series of light patterns and codings recognisable only to those who sail at sea.

A distinct architectural style and adaptation of fishing and shipping technologies are combined to provide a comfortable and familiar environment for the elderly. Levels down through the 'ship' – the hull, deck and hold – relate metaphorically to those of the merchant vessel. The boating lake is a microcosmic ocean on deck, by which the memory pathways of the elderly are kept open through the association of the miniature boats on a tiny sea. An 'alephographic' drawing – inspired by Jorge Luis Borges – sees everything as revealing the technologies and analogies that exist within the vessel.

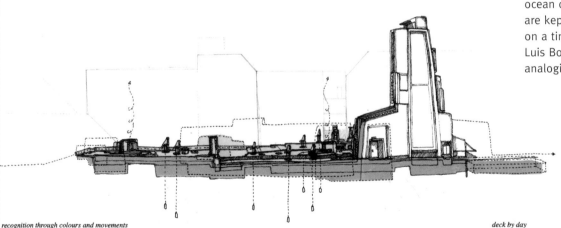

recognition through colours and movements

deck by day

recognition through lights and codes

deck by night

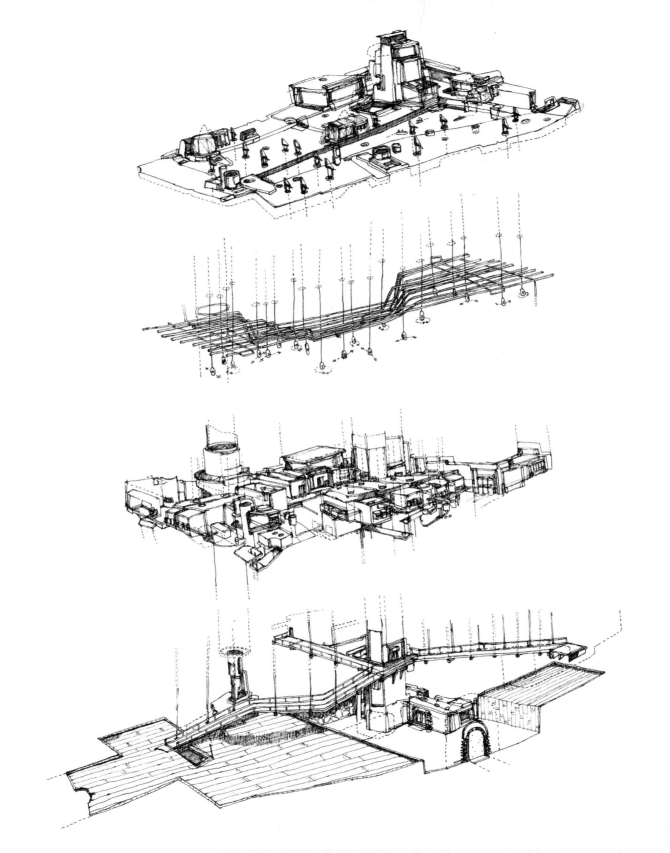

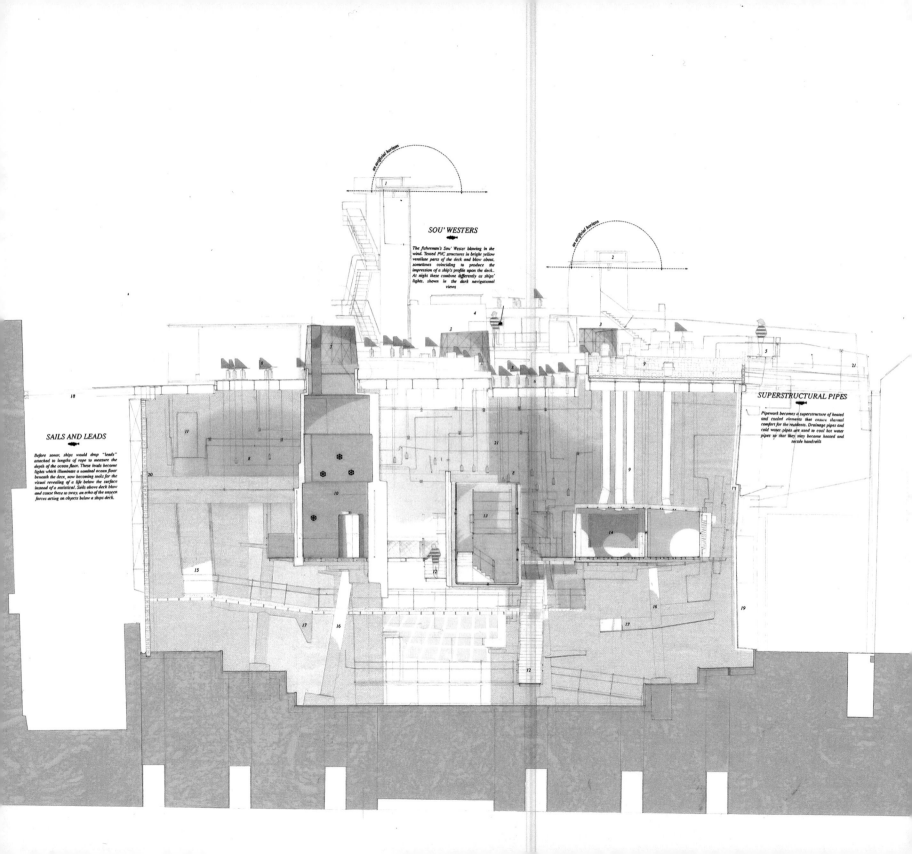

an artificial horizon

an artificial horizon

SOU' WESTERS

The fisherman's Sou' Wester blowing in the wind. Tented PVC structures in bright yellow ventilate parts of the deck and blow about, sometimes coinciding to produce the impression of a ship's profile upon the deck. At night these combine differently as ships' lights, shown in the dark navigational views

SUPERSTRUCTURAL PIPES

Pipework becomes a superstructure of heated and cooled elements that ensure thermal comfort for the residents. Drainage pipes and cold water pipes are used to cool hot water pipes so that they may become heated and tactile handrails

SAILS AND LEADS

Before sonar, ships would drop "leads" attached to lengths of rope to measure the depth of the ocean floor. These leads become lights which illuminate a nominal ocean floor beneath the deck, now becoming tools for the visual revealing of a life below the surface instead of a statistical. Sails above deck blow and cause these to sway, an echo of the unseen forces acting on objects below a ships deck.

Robert Street Cabinet

Umut Yamac
Diploma Architecture (2005)
Tutors: *Bob Sheil, Zoe Smith* and *Graeme Williamson*

The blue plaque scheme is run by English Heritage to 'celebrate great figures of the past and the buildings they inhabited'. This particular plaque lists writers James Barrie, Thomas Hood and John Galsworthy and architect Robert Adam as occupants of the address over a century. The 'Robert Street Cabinet' explores the layered occupation of the site and the relationships between the individuals. The project follows a series of imaginary letters between the author and said eminent figures as a means to piece together the details of this layered occupation. These written words form the basis for a series of physical constructs or drawing machines, placed in a third floor room once occupied by JM Barrie. Through movement, materiality and reference to the accompanying text, the machines interpret the street's past. The project questions whether the past and heritage can be recalled, revealed or displayed through anything but subjective assemblage.

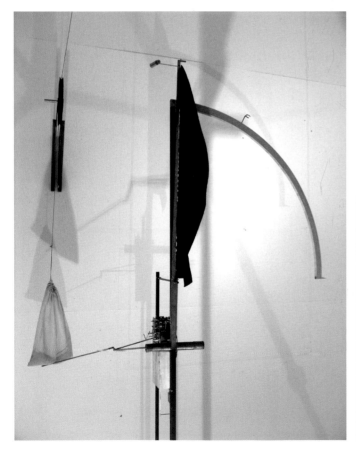
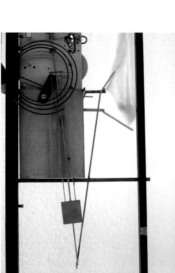

Salammbô

Martha Markopoulou
MArch Architectural Design (2006)
Tutor: *Phil Watson*

Based on the novel *Salammbô* by Gustave Flaubert, the project explores possible relations between language and architecture. Specifically, it examines how an architectural system can embody a novel's narrative and syntax, and how a physical reality might be constructed from this same novel. Architecture is thus conceived as the physical body of a 'fluid text'. A series of softly oscillating devices translate in space and time the conditions found in the narrative of *Salammbô*, enacting new points of view and changes of direction, speed, perspective and scale. The barbaric aesthetic reveals the exotic beauty that exists in *Salammbô*'s world of literature.

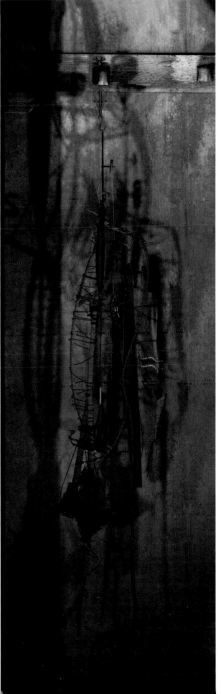

Salt Youth Hostel, Utah

James Daykin
Diploma Architecture (2005)
Tutors: *Niall McLaughlin* and *Yeoryia Manolopoulou*

The hostel is situated in the changeable alluvial soils to the north of the Great Salt Lake in Utah, at the boundary between desert and lake, where an infertile yet productive land meets the scaleless and infinite. The building, conceived as a monolithic earthwork, breathes in, absorbs and collects water from the environment during long uninhabited periods. It then releases water as necessary when visitors arrive. Individual rooms are made from salt as well as wax, felt and copper. Material processes register the change of seasons and inhabitation and, over time, deposits accumulate and root the building more firmly in its surroundings.

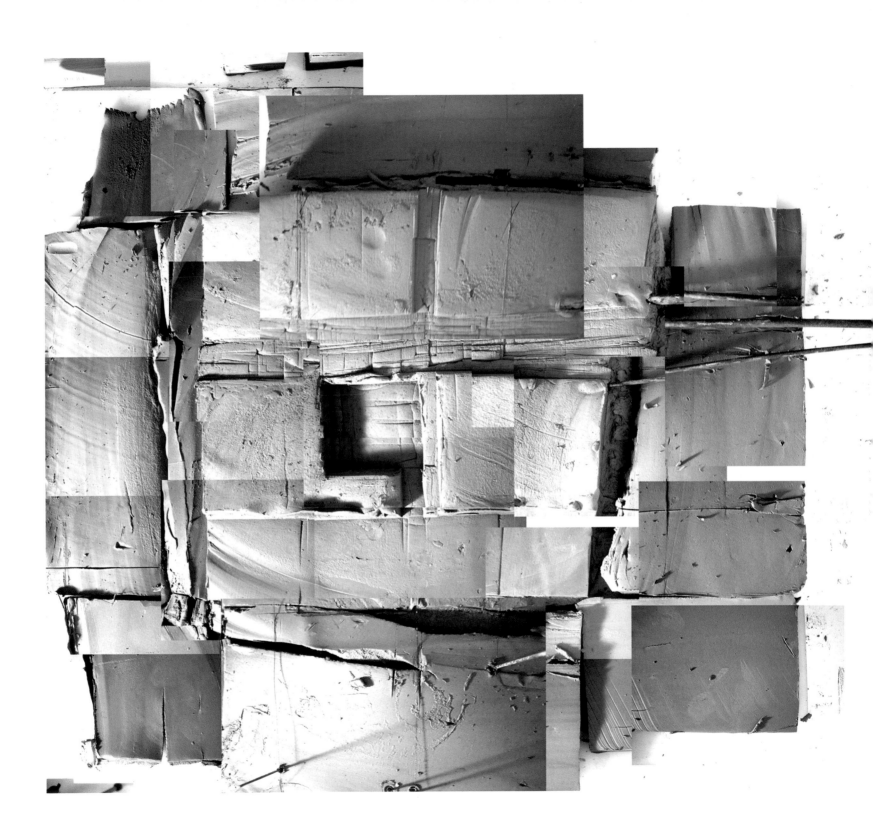

Scape

Eva Christina Sommeregger
MArch Architectural Design (2007)
Tutor: *Nic Clear*

'Scape' is a series of continuous journeys exploring the restlessness of a cyber-nomad, from mountain to forest and from desert to wasteland. An embodied camera occupies disembodied realities, getting rid of watching the moving body, and becoming the moving body. The project alludes to a non-object-based architecture of movement – formless and time-based – the intention being to create space from a 'nomocentric' viewpoint (360° x 360°), using a technique akin to Google's street view. Rather than generating sculptural shapes, 'Scape' mixes photography and computer animation to create an ambience.

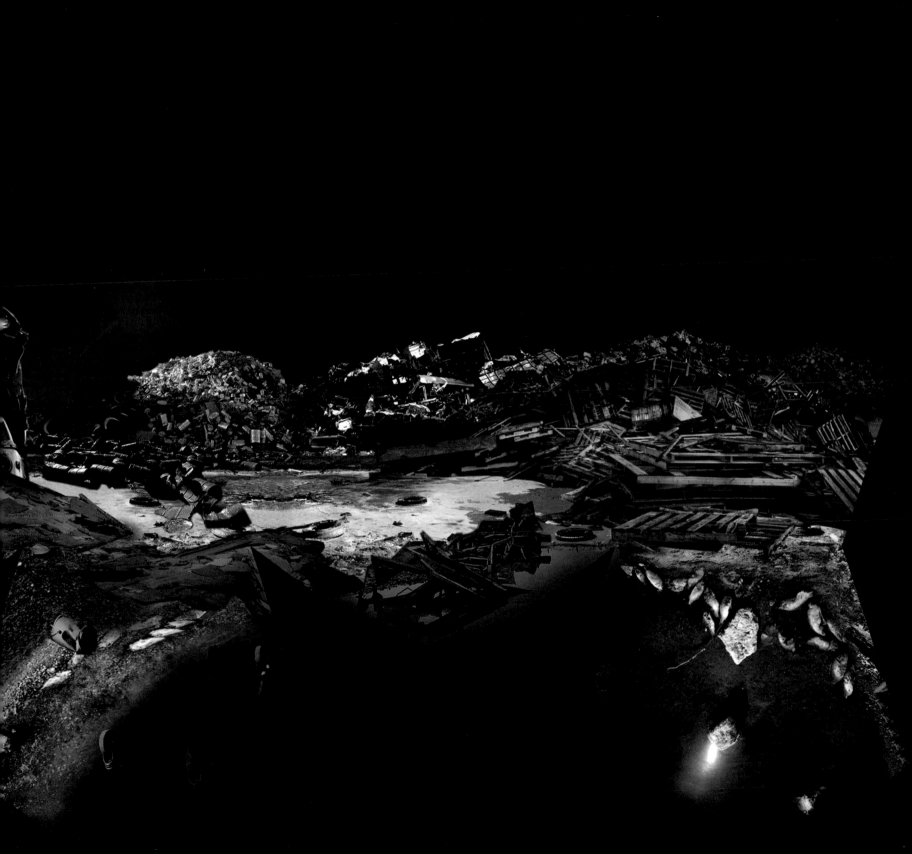

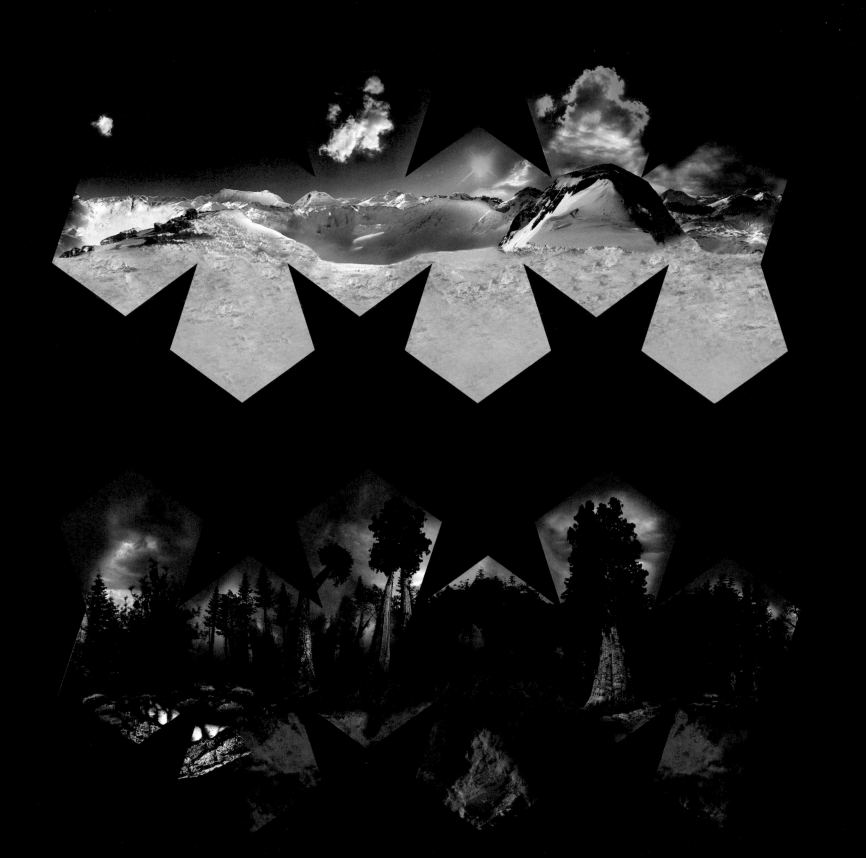

Scriptwriters' Retreat, Barcelona

Sarah Custance
BSc Architecture (2007)
Tutors: *Johan Berglund* and *Rhys Cannon*

The 'Scriptwriters' Retreat' is sited on the coastal edge of Barcelona. From this point, one is able to escape the city and look back in a moment of reflection. This is a place where a writer can be detached from the complexities of the urban landscape and find solitude. Elements of the building gradually fragment due to corrosion, so it progressively gets pushed over the boundary of Barcelona and into the drifting sea. As this occurs, the building shifts, creating a non-segregated, boundless space, an area for one to retreat from the city, sit and contemplate. Public and private areas therefore are at first separate, yet, as materials degrade, the line between them becomes increasingly blurred, confusing the hierarchy between observers and their subjects of study.

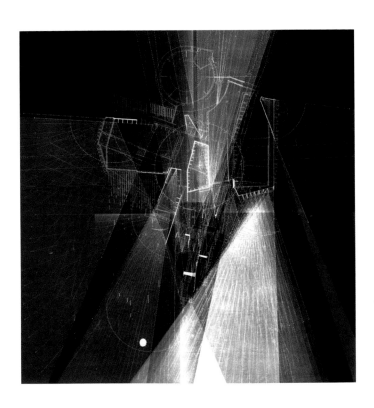

Seismological Research Centre, Porto

John Craske
BSc Architecture (2005)
Tutors: *Penelope Haralambidou, Eduardo Rosa* and *Sabine Storp*

Translating the shipping forecast for the North Sea in to a series of design instructions for interventions on the rooftop of a terrace house, the 'Seismological Research Centre' explores the disjuncture between intention and result in architectural design. Set in Porto, the project provides support to the national network of seismological stations and illustrates a volatile relationship between building and landscape. An ambitious proposition for a remote site, the scheme is not limited to the present. It embodies the layered history of the site, the slow remodelling of the landscape, the prospect of sudden change and future measured decay.

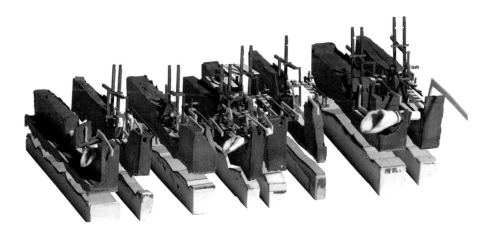

Ship Cultivation, Epping Forest, London

Christian Kerrigan
Diploma Architecture (2007)
Tutors: *Neil Spiller* and *Phil Watson*

The 'Ship Cultivation' project is predicated on the fact that if one puts metal corsets around growing trees, this will encourage timber to grow with a higher density, making it more effective in construction. Furthermore, this extreme bonsai technique can use other technologies – such as nanotechnology – within sections of trees, creating compositions of as-yet-unseen objects that can grow and be cultivated. In short, the project harvests the growth imperative of trees – particularly a yew tree copse (the subject of Kerrigan's extensive technical treatise) – to grow a ship.

The project has a 200-year life span, during which the copse, ship and launching pier are all grown. But what might be the effect if, during this germination period, a radical change of brief were to be enforced? The project therefore also considers what could happen if at around the, say, 150-year stage, the ships were no longer of use and the system had to be harnessed to create an obelisk. How might this be achieved, using the partially formed ship timbers? How would the system rearticulate itself to achieve these new ends? From a theoretical point, therefore, this project is about a synthesis of the natural and the artificial, and the potential of an architecture of parts that makes another architecture; it is an architecture before an architecture, fuelled by the natural power of growth.

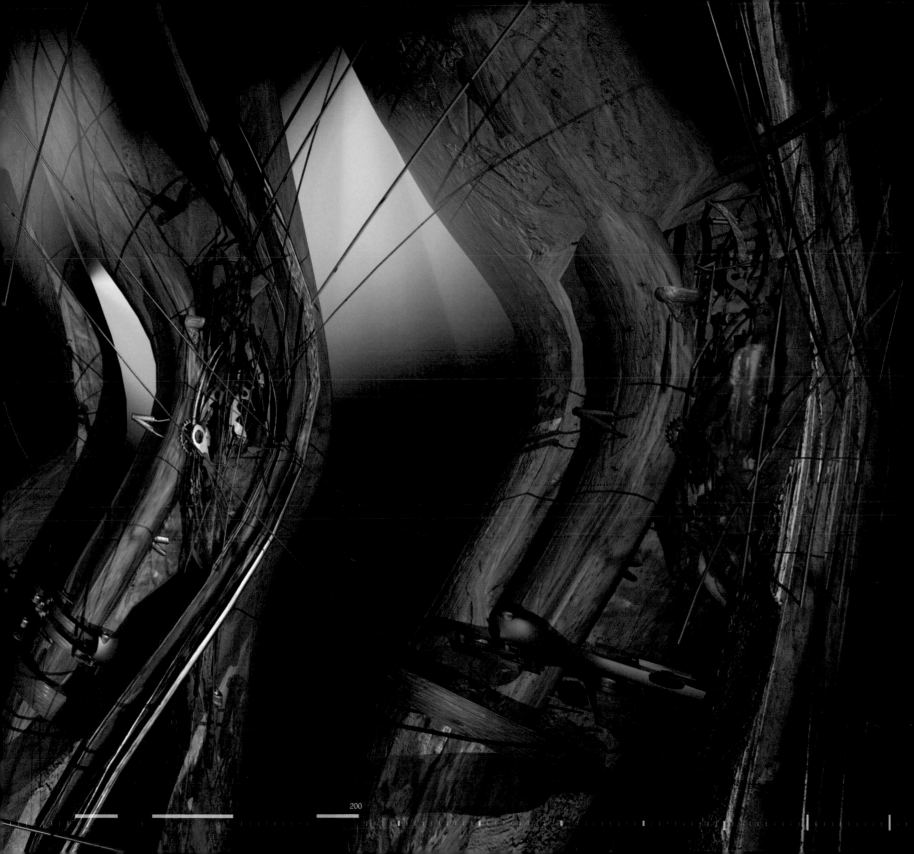

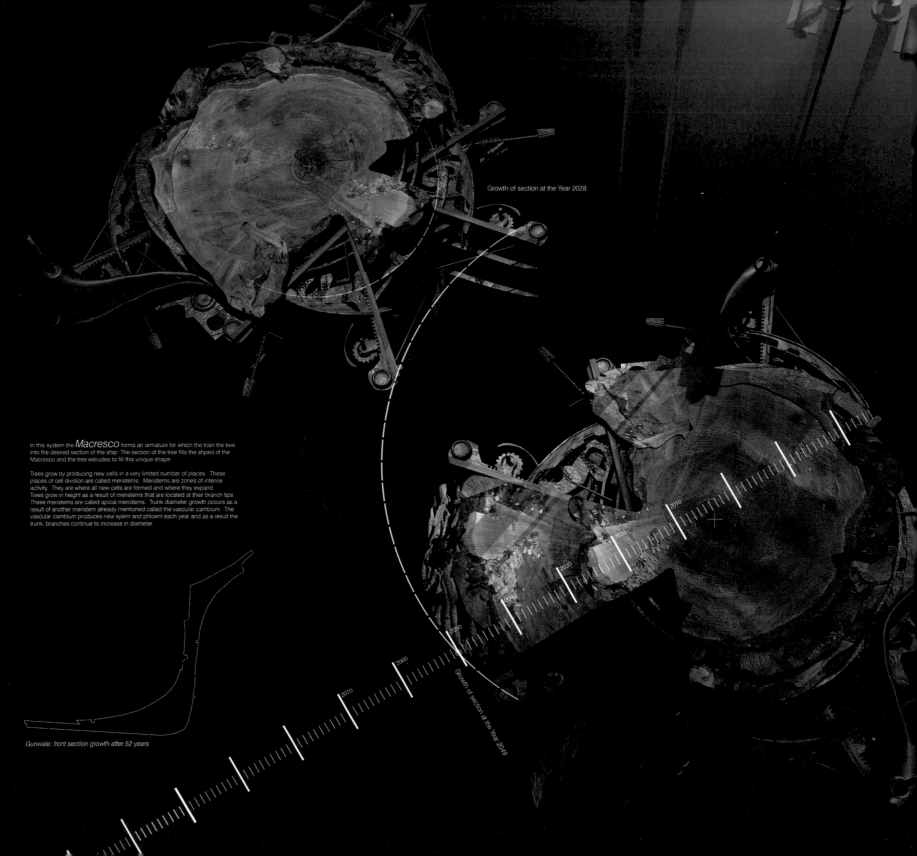

Growth of section at the Year *2028*

In this system the *Macresco* forms an armature for which the train the tree into the desired section of the ship. The section of the tree fills the shped of the Macresco and the tree extrudes to fill this unique shape

Trees grow by producing new cells in a very limited number of places. These places of cell division are called meristems. Meristems are zones of intense activity. They are where all new cells are formed and where they expand. Trees grow in height as a result of meristems that are located at their branch tips These meristems are called apical meristems. Trunk diameter growth occurs as a result of another meristem already mentioned called the vascular cambium. The vascular cambium produces new xylem and phloem each year and as a result the trunk, branches continue to increase in diameter.

Gunwale: front section growth after 52 years

Growth of section at the Year 2049

Social Club and Distillery

John Oliver
Diploma Architecture (2005)
Tutor: *Christine Hawley*

The site is next to Blackfriars Bridge, in a historic part of London. Within the project shell is a members' club that challenges the typical stereotype of neoclassical conformity often associated with such facilities. An almost cathedral-like sense of grandeur is created, using vast sculptural forms to defy the orthodoxy of standard floor-to-floor heights and the known relationship to doors and windows. Eating and serving are housed within forms abstracted from copper stills, hence imposing geometry. This geometry is then repeated at a different scale and at a higher level, where a small sequence of rooms hang across the walkways and social spaces. For all its internal theatricality, the building exercises external discretion, and the internal flamboyance is only occasionally glimpsed behind a facade of rectitude. The architectural experience is of gradual disclosure and surprise.

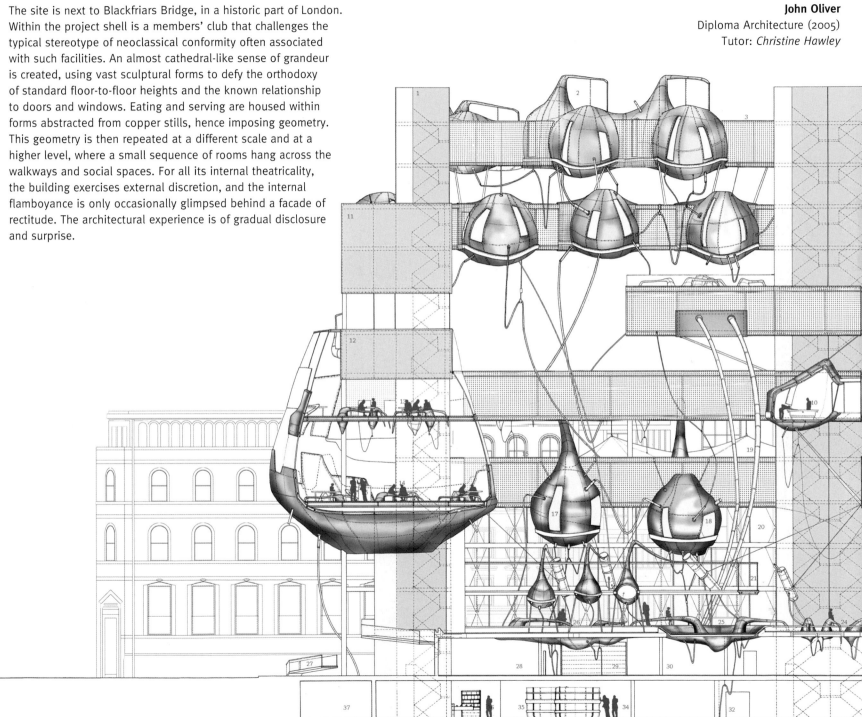

Sonic Feedback Machine

Richard Roberts
Diploma Architecture (2007)
Tutors: *Phil Ayres, Stephen Gage* and *James O'Leary*

This sound installation uses human presence and the reconfiguration of space to modify a self-generated analogue acoustic output. The resulting spectral music can be experienced by two classes of observer: the person who is instrumental in changing the acoustic architecture, and those who observe the transformation from a distance. In both cases, the specific transformations have to be learned before they can be enjoyed.

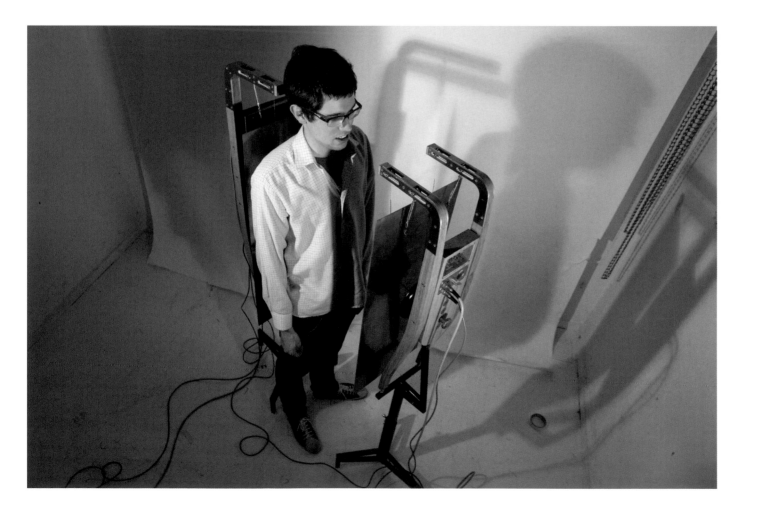

Spectral Turn Around Venice

Luke Jones
BSc Architecture (2008)
Tutors: *Ben Campkin, Max Dewdney,*
Penelope Haralambidou and *Chee-Kit Lai*

This design project and associated history and theory essay both critically question, with a quiet thoughtfulness and humour, John Ruskin's argument in *The Stones of Venice*. By designing spaces which exemplify Ruskin's virtues of architecture – Savageness, Changefulness, Naturalism, the Grotesque, Rigidity and Redundance – a new architectural language is created which heightens the impression of the building as a 'ruin', that is, something the beauty of which is inextricably linked to its decline, to its visible dilapidation. The building ostensibly aims to revive Venice, but in fact reveals its decrepitude.

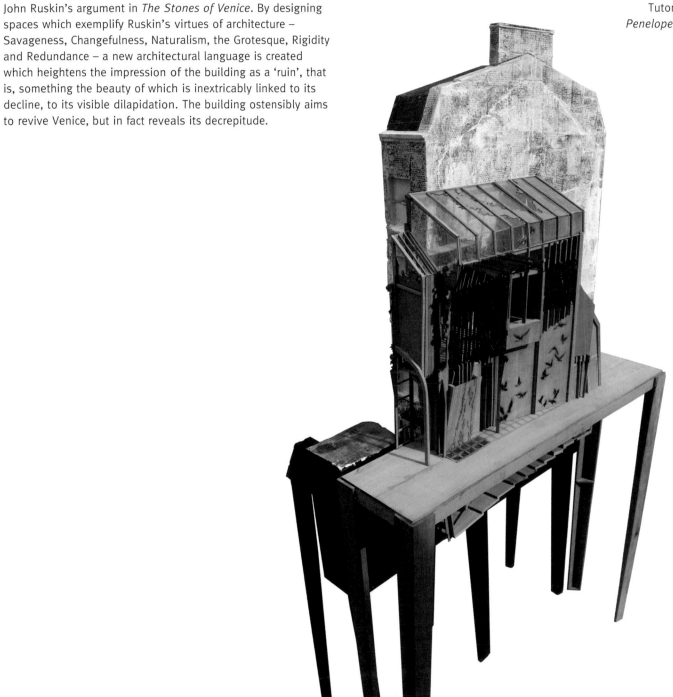

I spent several days, during a recent trip to Venice, in conversation with a ghost. The writer and critic John Ruskin became my spectral guide, and his commentary on the buildings that we visited transformed my experience of those spaces. What follows is an account of my time with him. This 'conversation' had the aim of finding a productive way of addressing Ruskin's difficult, extraordinary, vast *Stones of Venice* in light of the deeply, but incompletely, felt affection which many have for it.

The effect of invoking Ruskin in the manner of a haunting is not simply to convey a measure of sympathy for him or his work. Rather, I am trying to approach the subtle and intriguing way in which Ruskin's rhetoric, which is concerned with portraying contemporary Venice as a ruin, also starts to reveal within itself the ruin of Ruskin's ideals.

Torcello:

On the last day, Ruskin and I took the little-used boat that runs from Burano to Torcello, the abandoned medieval city on the northern fringe of the lagoon. From the top of its solitary campanile, Ruskin promised, 'we may command [...] one of the most notable scenes in this wide world of ours'. He described the building merging with its landscape; a landscape totally saturated in a kind of all-encompassing melancholy, 'a waste of wild sea moor, of a lurid ashen grey [...] lifeless, the colour of sackcloth [...] the corrupted sea water soaking through the roots of its acrid weeds.'[1] Its condition had become somewhat altered. The journey which Ruskin describes, up a 'narrow creek of sea [...] winding for some time among buried fragments of masonry' now takes place on foot, on a smart brick road, next to a fat, soapy channel of green water. From somewhere in the middle distance, the whine of a petrol generator can be heard. There are several recently-built houses, whose gardens are marked with a succession of chain-link fences.

We reached the cathedral and climbed the tower. From the top, a loud roaring sound could be heard. Towards the horizon, the salt marshes merged, in a grey haze, with the airport. The channels in the grey lagoon through which our ferry had travelled were marked with piles and buoys, which from the tower appeared to extend, without interruption, the geometry of the runways and taxiways out into the lagoon, almost to the shore of Torcello itself. I descended, filled with unease.

Reference
1   John Ruskin, *The Stones of Venice*, Smith, Elder & Co (London), 1873, p 11.

Stations of the Cross, St Ignatius of Loyola, Rome

Melissa Clinch
Diploma Architecture (2006)
Tutors: *Neil Spiller* and *Phil Watson*

Ideas of architectural anamorphosis are deployed to create a series of spaces and semiotics that inhabit the church of St Ignatius of Loyola, Rome, which has an anamorphic-painted ceiling and dome. From certain positions in the nave, the dome looks perfectly real; from other positions, the dome is revealed as a distorted painted form on the ceiling. This project positions three-dimensional forms within the church that create fluctuating architectural spaces according to the dynamics of the observer, and so operate like four-dimensional hypertexts. The spaces that are produced open and collapse as one moves, and so help the viewer to understand not only the science of anamorphic projection but also the rituals and history of the church.

Stolen Kiss

Fiona Sheppard
Diploma Architecture (2005)
Tutors: *John Puttick*, *Jane Rendell* and *Peter Szczepaniak*

This complex project – both designed and written – is based on the story of Peter the Great and his wife's love triangle at the Kadriorg Palace in Tallinn. The written thesis is a route through a series of architectural interventions designed in the palace, revealed over the course of a week. While the final design drawings and model provide viewpoints into this three-dimensional map of emotions, the writing frames the design project both theoretically and historically. The project explores psychoanalytic theories of love and desire, historical fact and invented fiction to create a tapestry of voices which suggest that the past, constructed through the present, has a spatial as well as chronological order.

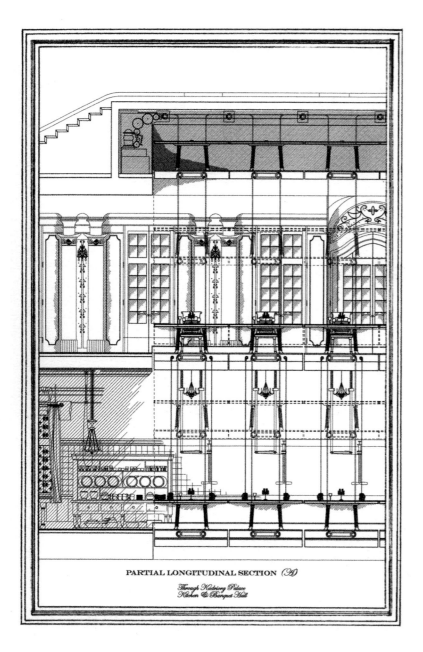

PARTIAL LONGITUDINAL SECTION (A)

*Through Kadriorg Palace
Kitchen & Banquet Hall*

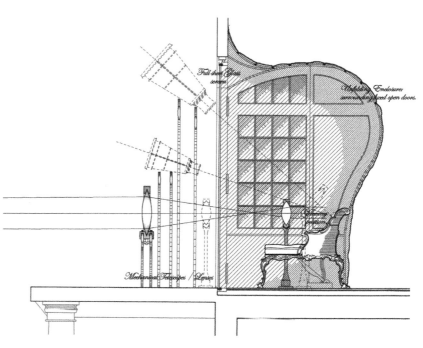

OBSERVATIONAL DIAGRAMS

Direction of The Look

Strange Ducks

Simon Kennedy
Diploma Architecture (2003)
Tutor: *Nic Clear*

A man finds a patent book on nanotechnology that magically comes to life from the page. The man goes through the book, and, despite its marvels, he ends up throwing it away. Witty and brilliantly executed, using fast-cut video and highly sophisticated animation and compositing, this short film brings to life the concepts of nanotechnology and self-replicating machines. It also demonstrates the gap between the potential, everyday reception and understanding of these technologies.

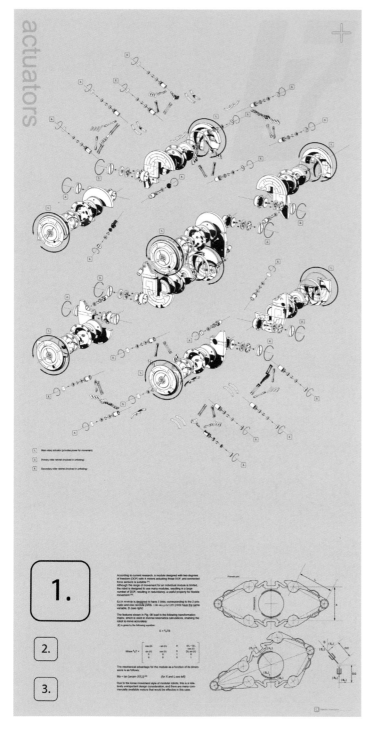

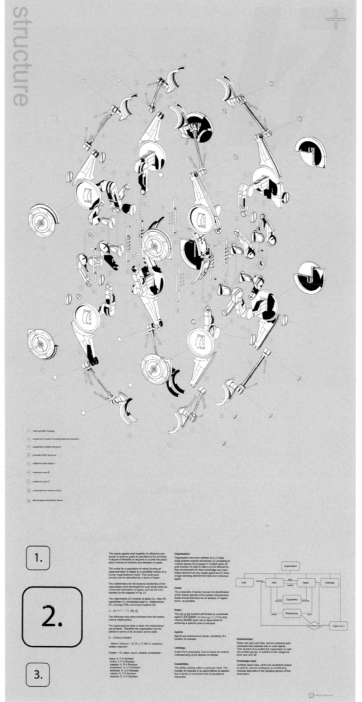

Symphonic Canon, Valletta

Pascal Bronner
BSc Architecture (2006)
Tutors: *Agnieszka Glowacka* and *Sabine Storp*

The building is an opera and theatre for the people of Malta. Resting atop the stony remains of the Royal Opera House in the city of Valletta, the project acts like a giant gramophone and megaphone, amplifying the orchestral sounds within on to adjacent streets and in to Freedom Square, which becomes the public auditorium. The building is also equipped with its own airship which, rising to heights that can be seen from far beyond the city walls, operates both as a symbol of celebration and as a silent church bell to draw in the crowds.

The architectural language is anachronistic, a strange and wonderful symbiosis of the archaic and the futuristic. Based on very astute observations of Valletta, the building opens up to, and addresses the city and its inhabitants, in a way that is both playful and appropriate.

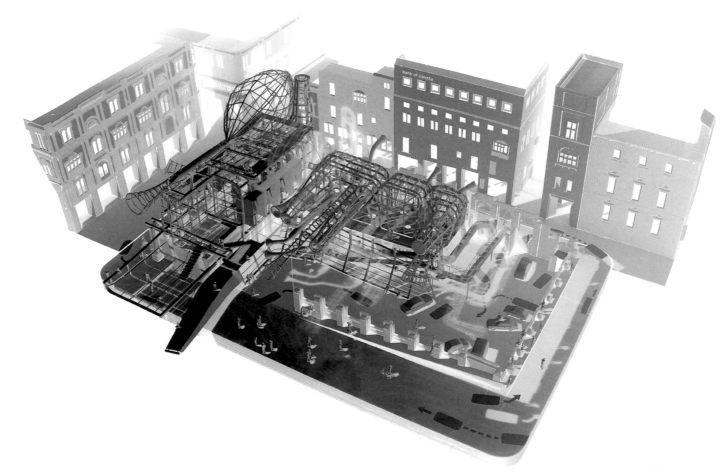

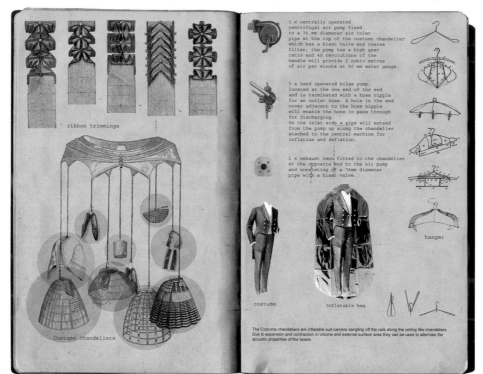

ribbon trimmings

Costume chandeliers

1 x centrally operated
centrifugal air pump fixed
to a 76 mm diameter air inlet
pipe at the top of the costume chandelier
which has a blast valve and coarse
filter, the pump has a high gear
ratio and 40 revolutions of the
handle will provide 2 cubic metres
of air per minute at 50 mm water gauge.

1 x hand operated bilge pump,
located at the one end of the end
and is terminated with a hose nipple
for an outlet hose. A hole in the end
cover adjacent to the hose nipple
will enable the hose to pass through
for discharging.
On the inlet side a pipe will extend
from the pump up along the chandelier
atached to the central machine for
inflation and deflation.

1 x exhaust vent fitted to the chandelier
at the opposite end to the air pump
and consisting of a 76mm diameter
pipe with a blast valve.

hanger

costume

Inflatable bag

The Costume chandeliers are inflatable suit carriers dangling off the rails along the ceiling like chandeliers.
Due to expansion and contraction in volume and external surface area they can be used to alternate the
acoustic properties of the space.

Sketchbook extract: The development of the costume chandelier

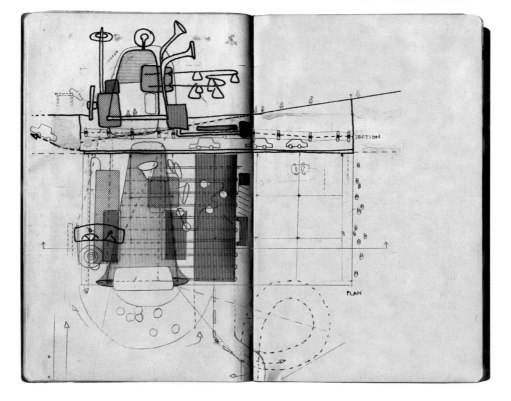

SECTION

PLAN

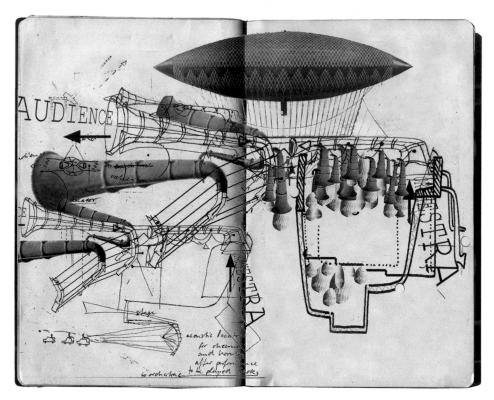

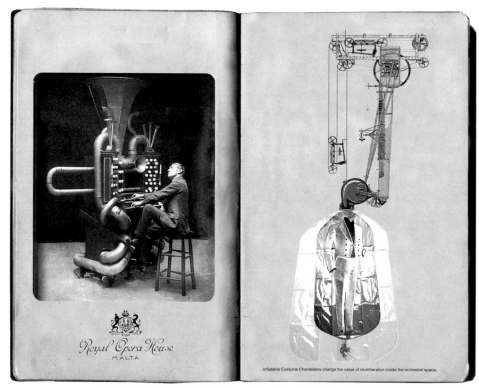

Inflatable Costume Chandeliers change the value of reverberation inside the orchestral space.

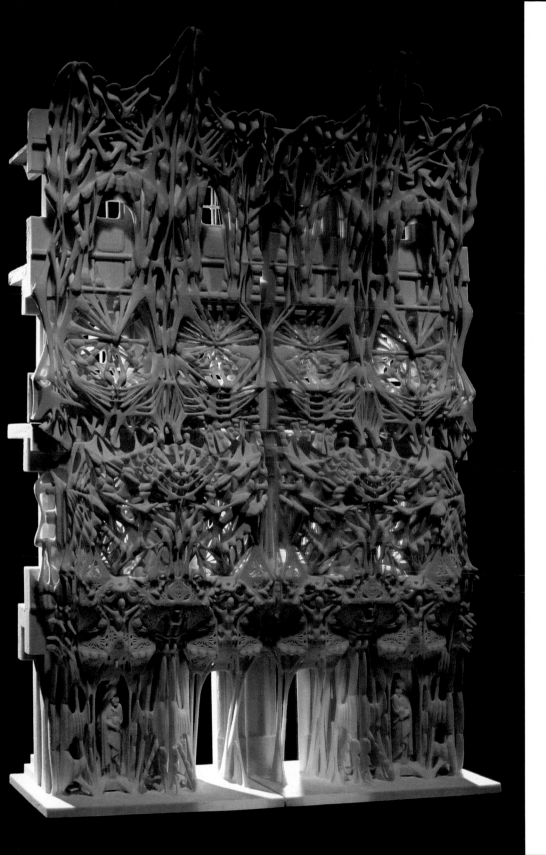

Synthetic Syncretism

Tobias Klein
Diploma Architecture (2006)
Tutors: *Marjan Colletti* and *Shaun Murray*

The narrative background for the 'Synthetic Syncretism' project is based on the Cuban religion of Santeria – a hybrid of Catholicism and African Yoruba tribal beliefs and animal sacrifices. Due to a lack of burial space in Havana, a ceremonial processional funerary route runs through the city. Slotted inside an existing cross-shaped courtyard, the inverted Chapel of Our Lady of Regla acts as this route's architectural highlight. Formal and structural expression is provided by a series of designed Santerian relics held inside the sacristy: skeletal and visceral utensils, three-dimensionally modelled and three-dimensionally printed to perfectly fit three-dimensionally scanned animal bones.

The project relies on a syncretism between contemporary CAD techniques and CAD-CAM technologies, informed by historical architectural references, site-specific design narratives and intuitive non-linear design processes. Digitally driven, the project combines dexterous modelling and rendering skills with creative invention and poetic thinking.

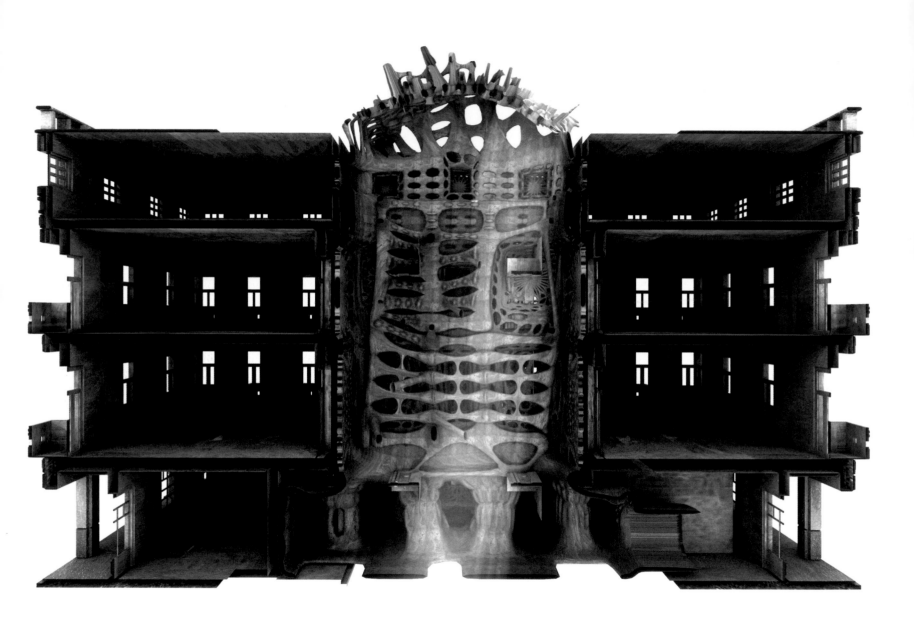

Textile Reading Room

Lucy Leonard
Diploma Architecture (2003)
Tutors: *Elizabeth Dow*, *Jonathan Hill* and *Jane Rendell*

The 'Textile Reading Room' written thesis evolved from the analysis of an antique kilim, which the author inherited from her maternal grandmother, with whom she had lived intermittently during the years preceding her grandmother's death in 2000. Through an explication of the kilim, ideas are extended about the ability of textiles to embody personal history and to question the concept of the architecture of home. Thus thinking about a specific personal textile led to using the textile as a way of thinking about architecture and deconstruction.

In this way, the dissertation itself becomes a textile construction where three books are worked around three textiles. With the first two books, the text is a response to the absent textile, and with the third text-textile pair, a cloth develops ideas in the text to produce both a re-working of all three books and the site for reading them.

The Graduation, UCL

Ian Laurence and **Karl Normanton**
Diploma Architecture (2006)
Tutors: *Phil Ayres, Stephen Gage* and *James O'Leary*

One way of achieving constant delight is to refer to those art forms that continually offer variety to the observer. These forms are often time-based and usually involve performance of one kind or another. Architecture has always provided a backdrop for social ritual and performance. Some architects, notably Inigo Jones, have investigated social performance directly through the creation of settings and costume. In this project, the structure of an institution and the nature of its iconic architecture are exposed to observers through the use of massive dance prostheses. This design is for one of seven such costumes prepared for a ritual engagement between UCL's faculties.

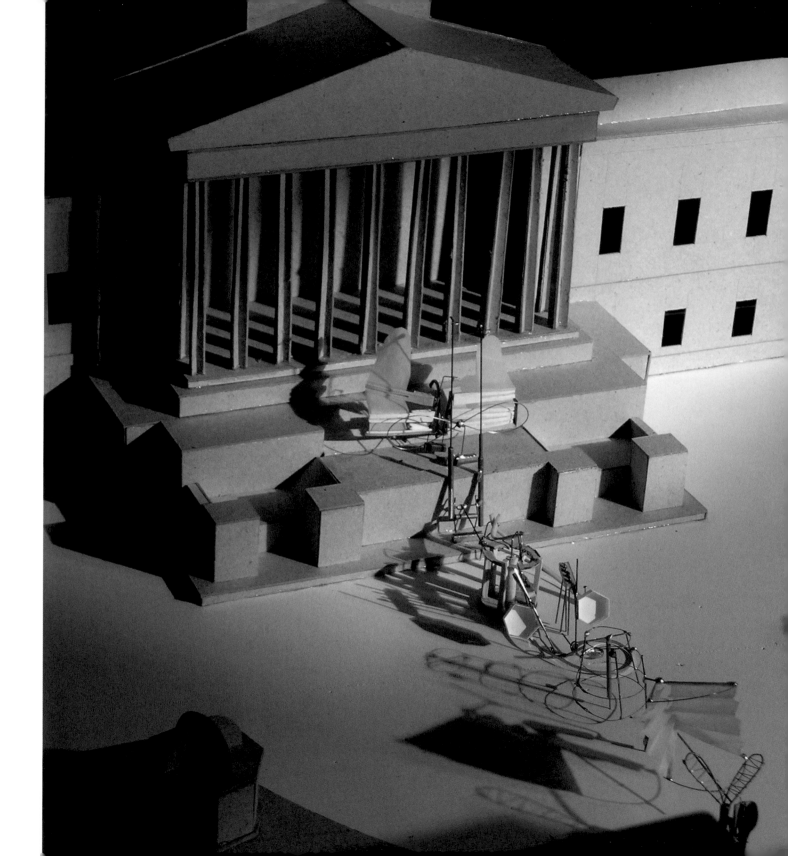

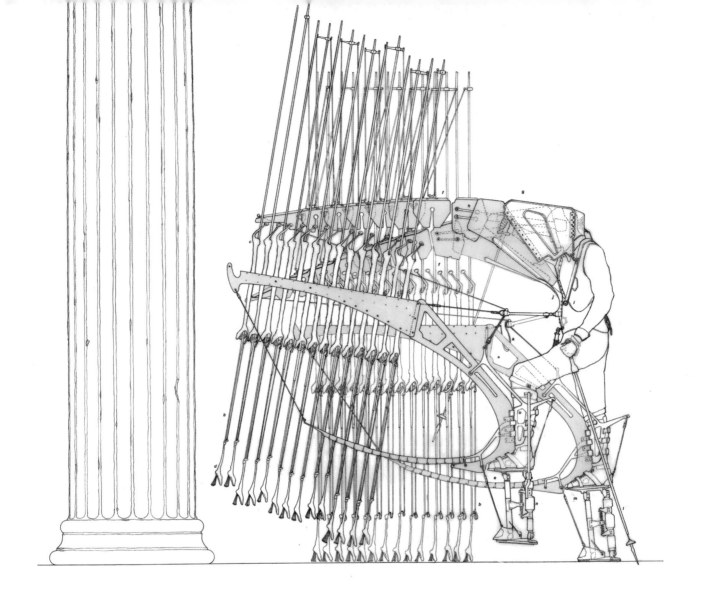
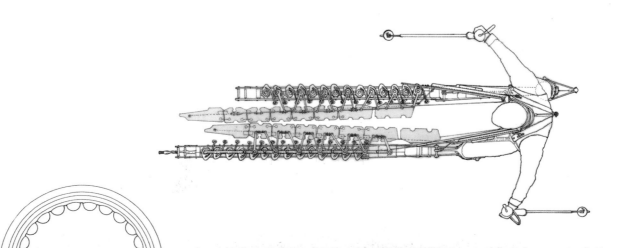

The Trial

Dan Brady
Diploma Architecture (2003)
Tutors: *Colin Fournier, Jane Rendell* and *Peter Szczepaniak*

The project is an architectural construction of Franz Kafka's *The Trial*, exploring how writing can be the motive for design through translation, from text to architecture. In Kafka's novel, architectural spaces are little discussed, yet K's struggle for redemption presents the reader with an intensely spatial experience. The challenge is therefore to translate the experience of Kafka's novel into concrete spaces. In this project, writings, drawings, photography and models are used to collectively represent Kafka's novel as architecture: an architectural translation takes the form of a book, broken down into separate chapters equivalent to those in *The Trial*; a 1:50 grey cardboard model represents the scenic architecture of The Trial; 1:1, face-to-face details of *The Trial* – the intimate spaces, interactions and objects – are the atmospheric details; Process Flow Diagrams translate the action of *The Trial* into diagrammatic drawings; and performative details are drawings of the rooms, spaces or locations in *The Trial* at a scale of 1:10 and 1:20.

Therapeutic Park, Shanghai

Masaki Kakizoe and **Kenny Tsui**
Diploma Architecture (2005)
Tutors: *Marjan Colletti* and *Marcos Cruz*

Contemporary metropolises are often known for their rapid growth and for the endless reproduction of skyscrapers along their emerging skylines. Such visual extravaganzas, however, hide a significant amount of leftover plots that disrupt the city's cohesion at ground level. This project for a herbal research institute in the Lu Jia Zui Park of Pudong in Shanghai rethinks one such urban void, inserting a highly dynamic building in an unused spot of the city. A symbolic and topological reinterpretation of the ginseng root marks the conceptual premise for a series of connecting paths that structure the institute, and also contextualise it in the redesigned topography of the park. Each of these routes invites the public to engage with the herbal gardens, while generating different viewpoints in which the distant skyscrapers seem to shift in scale.

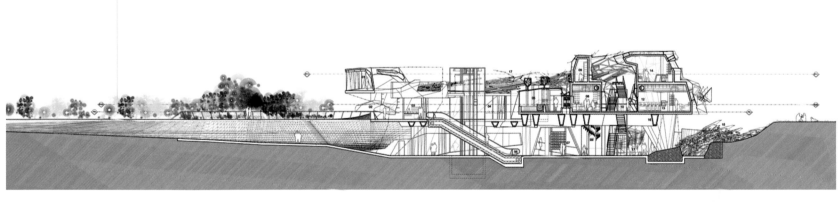

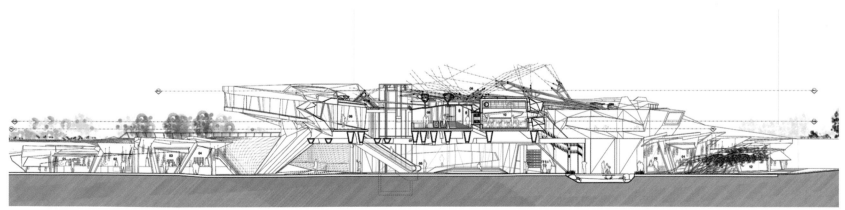

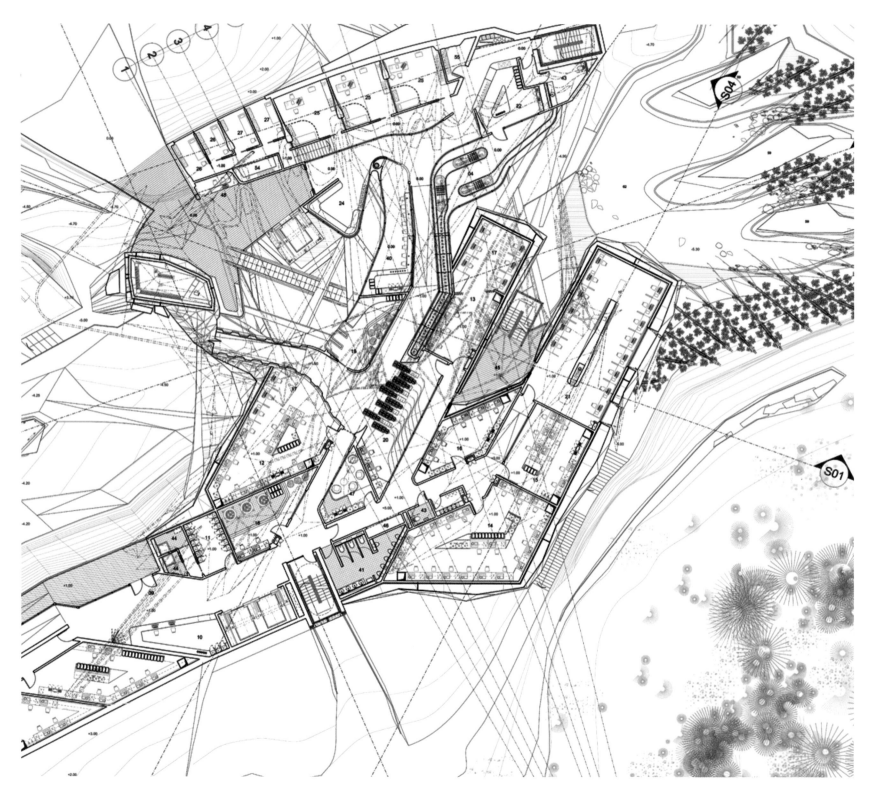

Times Square Tower, New York

Jonathan Mizzi
Diploma Architecture (2008)
Tutors: *David Ardill* and *Colin Fournier*

This project is a fusion of kinetic architecture with media display hardware and software systems. Sited in Times Square, the building entices visitors to take flight on an ephemeral journey up to a 360 degree view of Manhattan. Simultaneously these visitors are engaged in a cybernetic performance, with the square acting as a public auditorium, bringing the theatrics straight to the skin of the building. The project evolves Daniel Hirschman's art-based 'Glowbits' work into a three-dimensional skin that is immersive, interactive, reprogrammable and paramorphic. The tower creates an architecture that caters for the subjective response of the individual, directly engaging visitors in its constant mutations.

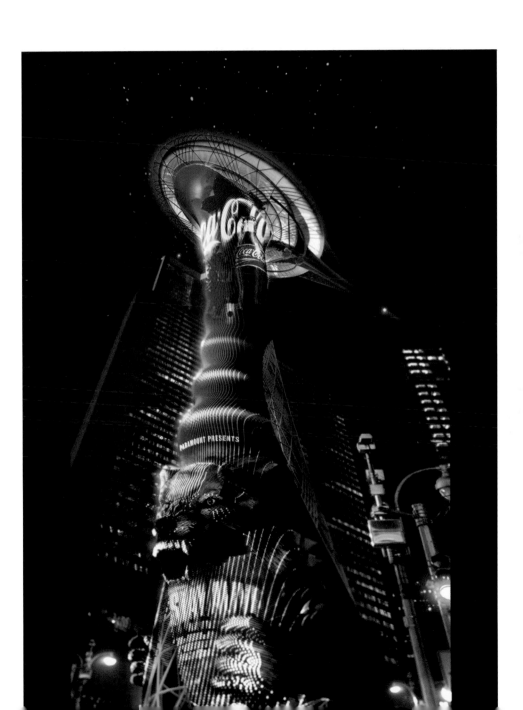

Toward a Material Poetics

Kristen Kreider
PhD Architectural Design (2008)
Supervisor: *Jane Rendell*

The aim of this practice-led PhD thesis is to develop a material poetics, informed theoretically. Cultivating a poetic practice in relation to fine art and spatial practice, Kreider originates a body of artworks including poetry, artist books, installation art, moving image and textual interventions into architectural and urban sites. Six art works are documented in this thesis, interlocking with five 'critical acts' that explore elements of poetic practice ('word', 'line', 'page', 'voice' and 'punctuation') in relation to materiality, spatiality and subjectivity.

From creative and critical practice emerges a triadic relation of intersecting concerns between 'sign', 'subject' and 'site' that are explored in theoretical writings. Arguing that formalist linguistic theory is capable neither of accounting for the material quality of the sign nor its relation to an object, the thesis cultivates an appreciation of the sign as an indexical symbol, in a material sense, as the basis for the sign in a material poetics. It then demonstrates how the material qualities of sign and site (including the materiality of the page, spatial context and body of the recipient) are integral to the ways in which meanings are generated and received.

The indexical symbol, in both a grammatical and material sense, underlies Kreider's theory of subjectivity in terms of a discursive and embodied relation between two speaking subjects, as 'I' and 'you', premised on 'voice' as an act of material spacing. Each art work and each critical act in this thesis reveals a different configuration of this complex intersubjective dynamic, ultimately offering a reconsideration of the lyric 'I' and 'voice' located at the crossover between contemporary poetry and text-based art practice.

Toy City, Shanghai

Nat Keast
Diploma Architecture (2005)
Tutors: *Marjan Colletti* and *Marcos Cruz*

The project explores the idea of toys as transitional objects, representing an intermediate area of experience between the internal and external imagination of a child or adult. The design, based around a community centre in Shanghai, stems from a series of intimate spaces of private cubbyholes proposed for an existing derelict facade, which are linked to establish dynamic multi-use community facilities. The building stimulates the imagination and develops an architecture that initiates imaginative engagement. Hence, an interwoven circulation system creates multiple 'childhood' perspectives of the interwoven, intricate, convoluted and immersive interior environments.

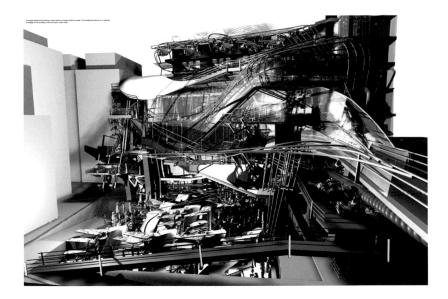

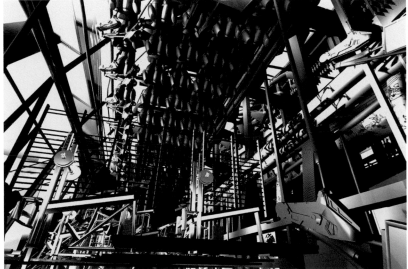

Tube Driver's House, Brighton

Dale Elliott
Diploma Architecture (2008)
Tutors: *Luke Lowings, Bob Sheil* and *Emmanuel Vercruysse*

This project posits an alternative to the hyper-acceleration of the digital age, and examines the damaging effects upon health and well-being through the fracture of solar, mechanical and chronological rhythms. The project is tailored around the lifestyle of an underground train driver, an interview with whom is incorporated into the accompanying thesis. The proposition is built around the driver's extreme, but not unusual, deprivations, and imagines how the strange regularity of her encapsulated existence may be realigned through core spatial and temporal phenomena. The project is developed through time-based chronological tools, escape mechanisms and adaptable spatial enclosures.

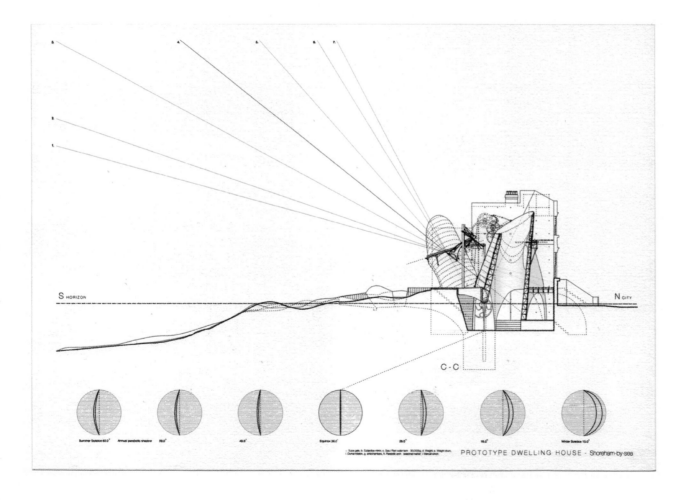

PROTOTYPE DWELLING HOUSE - Shoreham-by-sea

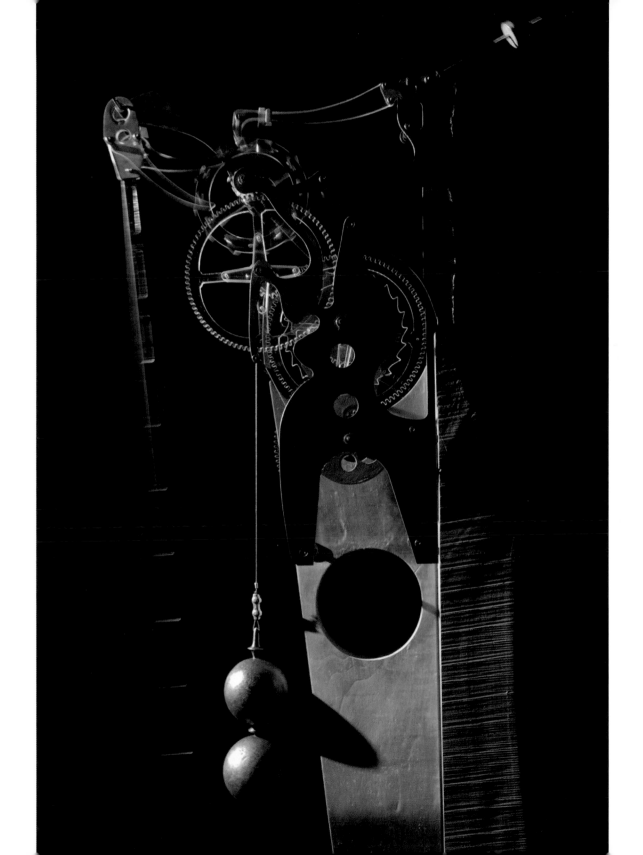

Tuneable City

Melissa Appleton
Diploma Architecture (2008)
Tutors: *Laura Allen* and *Mark Smout*

The 'Tuneable City', an analogue landscape, is constructed from interconnected radio receivers, microphones and amplifiers. The 'city' is inhabited by a responsive landscape, comprising elements entitled, for example, the 'brittle mist' and 'hanging orchard'. The whole scheme is brought to life by the saturated radio environment, movements accumulating from imperceptible vibrations to major oscillations that ripple onto the surface of the city.

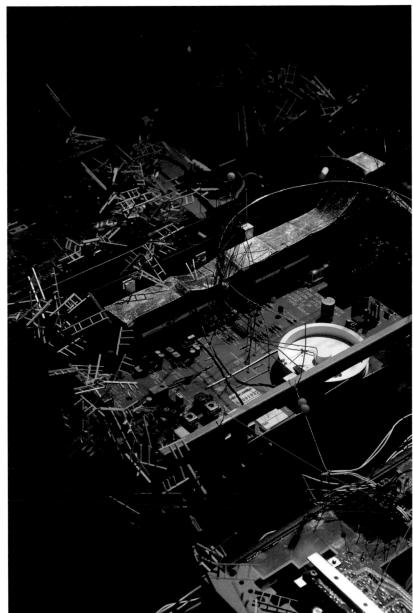

Twenty-Three Box Brownie Cameras

Daniel Swift Gibbs
BSc Architecture (2007)
Tutors: *Abigail Ashton* and *Andrew Porter*

For this second year BSc project, the students were asked to read a piece of text from Iain Banks's *The Wasp Factory* and to investigate aspects of collections, collectors and hoarders. Swift Gibbs collected a large number of Box Brownie cameras, and incorporated many of them within a portable photographic device.

Uncle Toby's Garden

Catherine Irvine
Diploma Architecture (2008)
Tutors: *Niall McLaughlin* and *Yeoryia Manolopoulou*

'Uncle Toby's Garden' is a literary world described in Laurence Sterne's novel *Tristram Shandy*. Uncle Toby, an injured war veteran, constructs a garden on the bowling-green behind his kitchen by re-enacting step-by-step the multiple sieges of Queen Anne's War (1702–13). The proposal incorporates All Hallows' Church and vicarage, Sutton-on-the-Forest, where Sterne resided and conceived of the eccentric Uncle Toby. A dreamscape inhabits the site topography with the fortifications of Namur, the typography of the novel, a field of Uncle Toby's fictional moments and Sterne's recorded site experiences. These layers are navigated and stitched together by attacks and retreats of the Siege of Namur. Sterne's deliberate 'anti-character sketch' of Uncle Toby inspires the elevation of architectural experience above architectural image or object.

238

Unfolding Mobile Architecture

Daniel Hall
BSc Architecture (2007)
Tutors: *Penelope Haralambidou* and *Eduardo Rosa*

This second year BSc project is inspired by the work of the artist Francis Alÿs. It comprises a series of images devoted to the itinerant street merchants of the Mexican megacity, who physically propel large pushcarts packed with merchandise as everyday ephemeral architecture. In response to Alÿs, this project is an unfolding mobile architecture: a large deployable structure, which, like a living creature, breathes and sheds parts of its 'feathered' skin as well as collecting new material to grow and transform. As an archive of lost letters, the project reframes an old tradition of scribes and letter writing in a new setting, a labyrinth of spaces with a Kafka-esque feel.

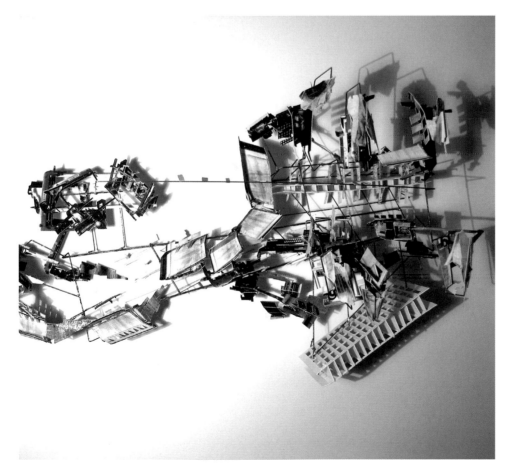

(Un)Natural History Society, London

Anton Ambrose
Diploma Architecture (2005)
Tutors: *Elizabeth Dow* and *Jonathan Hill*

The '(Un)Natural History Society' houses a research institute and its researchers. But rather than for people, this home is designed for, and inhabited by, the weather. There is a window for the wind, for example. As the building grows, it drifts further from the needs of people, blurring the boundaries between home and garden, work and rest, inside and outside, the natural and the artificial. But diminishing the home's association with utility and security is itself liberating, encouraging pleasurable and ad-hoc forms of inhabitation, so that we may inhabit a weathered home the way we do a weathered landscape.

Urbanisms

Nic Clear and **Iain Borden**

Minor Urbanisms

The conception of the modern city as rational, planned and functionally serviced has dominated many architectural histories and urban theories since the Enlightenment. Ideas of a scientific planning as the deterministic driver of growth and development address the functional needs of the city, while other requirements, such as pleasure, delight and happiness, are often neglected and, in some cases, completely ignored.

As many basic functional needs are met through legislation and technical innovation, the qualitative and experiential nature of the city needs to be addressed through other means. What makes a city pleasurable is not something that can legislated for, nor is it simply a matter of design and/or design strategies. Subjective notions of habitation can be best addressed through speculative projects that resist the totalising conceptions of formalist, or functionalist urbanism.

One aspect of the various 'urbanisms' that have grown out of the UCL Bartlett School of Architecture over the past few years is the movement away from totalising propositions, instead suggesting particular and often discrete transformations of the urban landscape, either through changes in the type of urban 'practices' that are performed by the various inhabitants, or through subtle transformations and augmentations of the technological infrastructure.

These approaches might be referred to, after Deleuze and Guattari's work on Kafka, as 'minor urbanisms', urbanisms that operate on the periphery of the urban discourse, often proposing speculative – even fanciful – solutions to mundane and prosaic questions.

The Everyday

The conceptions of the everyday – the quotidian – as developed in particular by Henri Lefebvre and Michel de Certeau have become highly influential as critical vectors in establishing alternative urban methodologies. This is with good reason, namely, the power of these concepts to suggest that the issue of the late-capitalist city is not simply to do with the material, the functional and the acquisitional, and that contemporary urbanisms should also be concerned with the experiential and qualitative expectations of the populace. Urban citizens are not simply passive consumers, but are constantly engaged with the city, appropriating and re-appropriating the sites and systems for their own ends. How an architecture might engage with such systems is explored in many of the projects – both designed and written – contained within *Bartlett Designs*.

Similarly, the influence of the various psychogeographical techniques of Unitary Urbanism as proposed by the Situationist International – the *dérive*, *détournement* and the primacy of *homo ludens* – maps out tactics to address an urban territory that resists the totalising functionalist concepts inherited from 'modernity'.

The concepts of the irrational, of play and the ephemeral are often found at the heart of many of the urban speculations constructed within Bartlett projects. This does not mean that the projects themselves are necessarily irrational and ephemeral, rather that the logic that underlies the project addresses a value system that is not prescriptive and reductive.

Performing the City

One of the most important concepts expressed in many Bartlett projects is the way in which students address the issue of the city as something that is performed or practised. Projects that deal with occupation often present this occupation as exceptional, and in many cases excessive, rather than assuming Taylorist norms. Such projects often focus on collaboration as one of their principal tactics, and bring ideas and techniques from other disciplines – dance, film and literature being the most obvious examples. While these ideas may seem a luxury in cities where poverty and marginalisation are still real issues, the point of such speculations is to suggest that even if the material needs of the populace are met, the urban condition has to address and promote values and forms of social organisation that are liberating and celebratory.

This focus on spatial practices rather than built form can be highly controversial, but a debate regarding the qualitative aspects of the built environment is something that has frequently been missing from a professional discourse that has too often almost completely sold itself to the chimeras of the 'free market', and to the idea that problems are solved by development alone, rather than addressing how people use or even misuse space.

Furthermore, the limitations of traditional systems of representation – which assume a fixed projection representing the fixed point of view of a static subject – are now contested through the use of interactive and time-based media, media that radically reconfigure the range of what falls under the scope of the architectural.

Future Urbanisms

The urbanisms of the 19th and 20th centuries were facilitated by forms of technological development that were large in scale, invasive and instrumental; technological innovation was primarily concerned with industrial production, the flows of organic material, either through assisted and unassisted forms of human circulation or by removing waste, and through the distribution of energy. All such systems tended to require an infrastructure that was highly visible and gave symbolic status to these technologies.

With the decline of cities as sites of production, the flows of the 21st century are just as likely to be concerned with information systems and telematics. These technologies often rely on invisible or hidden systems, their only visual component being the black boxes that do not celebrate their technological status in the same fetishistic manner of earlier 'machinic' technological disciplines. New forms of symbolic value are generated around the intersections of these technical systems with the existing material fabric, and the new aesthetic forms generated are rarely related to any recognisable type of functionalism. The interface has replaced the machine as the icon of the late capitalist city.

Issues of energy conservation and sustainability will mean that many of the products that have historically been shipped out of the city, especially energy and waste, will have to be recycled and reclaimed, and future urbanisms will require much greater levels of self-sufficiency and autonomy. And in a corresponding manner, the newer technological infrastructures of the information space of the near future will lack the same visible presence of their analogue forebears, and a new type of notation and representational system is now required.

While the programmatic aspects of such transformations can be clearly articulated, it is the effect of such transformations on inhabitation that projects need to address, through a new system of urban discourse.

At a time when basic survival is a primary issue for many inhabitants of urban centres in the developing world, this approach may seem indulgent, narcissistic and decadent. The type of issues facing the centres of late capitalism, however, are not simply concerned with basic survival, for what is required is a whole new conception of what the city is and what the city does. The answers to these questions are not simply to solve basic needs, but to re-address the whole idea of needs themselves.

The political will for the type of transformations now required to solve global inequality requires that those-that-have now develop a completely different attitude to what they do have, as well as to the way that this wealth – in all its forms – may be distributed. The urbanisms of the future need to possess a completely different type of vocabulary – and it is this vocabulary that is now one of the many speculations of the Bartlett.

Watching, Waiting

Alex McAslan
Diploma Architecture (2005)
Tutor: *Nic Clear*

Set in London Bridge train station, 'Watching, Waiting' brings together trainspotters, pigeons and commuters as they occupy the same space – though not necessarily the same place and time. The film depicts an uncanny vision of the everyday, as time freezes and the surrounding architecture begins to take on the flocking characteristics of the station's inhabitants. Using digital video, digital photography and complex post-production techniques, this evocative 'cinematic' piece constructs virtual models of the actual buildings of London Bridge, and consequently allows the creation of a series of 'impossible' shots.

Weights and Measures Institute: le Concombre

Gregory Jones
Diploma Architecture (2004)
Tutors: *Simon Herron* and *Susanne Isa*

The central tenet in this project is the development of an alternative unit of measure, drawing inspiration from ISO 9000 and Marcel Duchamp's *Three Standard Stoppages*, a rejection of the SI metre, to be replaced with the universal *concombre* (cucumber). In line with the inherent fragility of the metre, errors are taken as an essential prerequisite, as the fundamental building blocks for the institute in refining new technologies of measurement and verification. The institute has to maintain the certainty of the standard; each regularised ideal specimen stays at its optimum size for three days, and multiple growth systems ensure that there is always a perfect specimen in place.

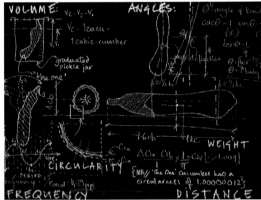

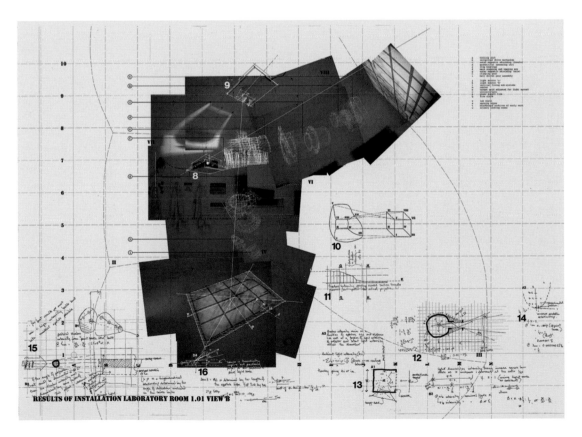

RESULTS OF INSTALLATION LABORATORY ROOM 1.01 VIEW B

Whale House, Madeira

Aaron Lim
BSc Architecture (2006)
Tutors: *Laura Allen*, *Rhys Cannon* and *Mark Smout*

The project is for a guesthouse in an abandoned whaling community at Caniçal, Madeira. A whale is washed ashore, hollowed, unfolded and exposed to a shifting climate: precipitation, which is frequent, and the wind. Travellers unload suitcases into blubber walls, dispose of dirty laundry in folded blubber cavities that protrude from its underbelly, and tend to weeds growing in cells tucked in the skin using saturated blubber. The whale building charts and records the mysterious lives of temporary residents, and reveals them to the denizens of Caniçal, who are fond of whaling and the sea but can no longer hunt.

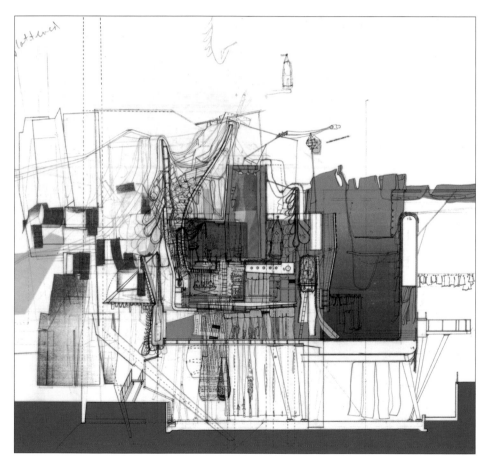

Josie Kane
PhD Architectural History and Theory (2007)
Supervisor: *Iain Borden*

The PhD thesis 'A Whirl of Wonders! British Amusement Parks and the Architecture of Pleasure, 1900–39' is the first historical study to define, document and interpret the amusement park landscape in Britain. The research raises a number of questions about shifting notions of pleasure and new attitudes towards technology and, in doing so, contributes to a developing interdisciplinary field which seeks to identify more adequately the experience of modernity, architecture and design.

The amusement parks, which first appeared in England at the turn of the 20th century were startlingly novel and complex, combining fantasy architecture, new technology, ersatz danger, spectacle and mass consumption in a new collective experience. This entertainment formula marked a radical departure in terms of visual, experiential and cultural meanings. The huge, socially-mixed crowds flocking to the new parks did so purely in the pursuit of pleasure, which the amusement parks commodified in exhilarating new guises. Between 1906 and 1939, nearly 40 major amusement parks operated across Britain. By 1939, millions of people visited these sites each year. The amusement park had become a defining element in the architectural and psychological pleasurescape of Britain.

At three key sites – Blackpool Pleasure Beach, Dreamland in Margate, the Kursaal at Southend – new understandings of 'pleasure' were forged for mass audiences, in which mechanically produced multi-sensory stimulation or thrill was central. The heady mix of rides, side-shows and crowds combined to create a visceral spectacle in which people suspended the behavioural constraints of everyday life. The amusement parks, therefore, offered a landscape in which people encountered modernity in a new and intensely physical manner.

In the early 1900s, the appropriation of technology for respectable mass pleasure was a defining and decisive moment in the experience of popular modernity. The mechanical pleasures were modern: creating a new heterogeneous social space for technology, also in the particular kinaesthetic experiences produced. In the later interwar years, the experience of popular modernity in Britain was increasingly qualified by the discourse of 'new leisure' and allied Modernist design principles. 'Being modern' came to be explicitly visual as well as experiential and, at the most successful parks, the modern aesthetic superseded technology as the prime vehicle for expressing modernity.

Whisky Distillery, Arizona

Richard Hardy
BSc Architecture (2006)
Tutors: *Julia Backhaus* and *Pedro Font Alba*

Situated on the shore of Lake Mead in Arizona, a whisky distillery forms the centre of a self-sustainable community. Driven by the water opportunities in this part of the Mojave Desert, it encourages the cultivation of barley on fertile ground. Constructed with physical fragments taken from nearby aeroplane scrapyards, the proposal celebrates the design value of recombining found parts into new assemblies, where meaning is subverted within, and rediscovered through, extraordinary new spaces.

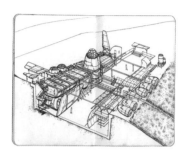

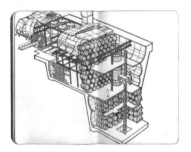

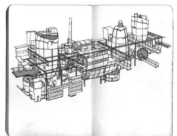

Olivia Gordon
Diploma Architecture (2004)
Tutor: *Jane Rendell*

This thesis uses the famous section of CS Lewis's *The Lion, the Witch and the Wardrobe* – where Lucy enters the wardrobe and first discovers Narnia – as an index for a personal storage system. The text is used to house a personal narrative on the theme of closet space, an individual 'wardrobe of words'. The writing, then, in inhabiting the 'fixed' text of Lewis's novel, uses the predetermined structure of the story to develop a personal investigation on the theme of cupboards. In effect the aim is to, like Lucy, enter the mundane space of the wardrobe and discover a 'whole country' within.[1]

The methodology used is similar to that used by Georges Perec in his essay 'Think/ Classify' where he explains: 'The alphabet used to "number" the various paragraphs of this text follows the order in which the letters of the alphabet appear in the French translation of the seventh story in Italo Calvino's *If On A Winter's Night a Traveller*'.[2] In 'Wordrobe', however, the words of a chosen extract, rather than letters, are used as a means of classification. In effect, the reading and writing between the confined lines of the text, a 'slotting between' as one would file objects away in a cupboard, becomes a means of generating a spacious place of creative investigation.

It is from within this process of writing, where the method of classification is so obtuse that it questions the opposition of orderly classification versus random spontaneous thought, that the theme of the writing itself develops. This is, namely, an exploration of the nature of the space of the closet, both as a mechanism for control or categorisation and also as a place for the freedom of the imagination. And so, in following Lucy's journey from exterior to interior, the discussion investigates these alternate themes and then reflects on the implications that such a duality might have for the architect as designer and definer of space.

References
1 CS Lewis, *The Lion, the Witch And the Wardrobe*, HarperCollins (London), 1950, p 63.
2 Georges Perec, *Species Of Spaces And Other Pieces*, Penguin Books (London), 1997, p 204.

Summer Show

The Summer Show is the annual celebration of work at the UCL Bartlett School of Architecture. Over 450 students show innovative drawings, models, devices, texts, animations and installations. Every year, over 15,000 people visit the exhibition, including representatives from many of the top names in the world of architecture.